WORK THE BUGS OUT!

PRACTICES TO WORK IN, & ON, YOUR BUSINESS

WENDY DICKINSON

Illustrated by
JEREMY YEE

Dickinson, Wendy. *Work the Bugs Out! Practices To Work In, & ON, Your Business.*

Copyright © 2021 by Wendy Dickinson

Published by KWE Publishing: www.kwepub.com

ISBN 978-1-950306-48-0 (hardback) 978-1-950306-49-7 (ebook)

Library of Congress Control Number: 2020906141

1. Entrepreneurship (Books) 2. Business Leadership 3. Business & Organizational Learning

PREFACE

Wendy Dickinson

My Dad was a "maker." He worked as a union iron worker for years. Once the crew spent more time on strike than on the job, he left to start his own construction company. My Dad had no business experience, and it hurt him. He knew a few people who had businesses and took a chance. He learned so much, and had a great time with his subcontractors, but ultimately it wasn't enough. It all came tumbling down when an owner delivered a change order, agreed to the increased costs with a handshake agreement, and then refused to pay the additional charges. My Dad lost his business, his confidence, and his pride.

It was painful to watch and to experience as a family. That wasn't the last time that family members chose to start businesses that became jobs, not assets. When those family members were ready to retire, my husband JD had the unpleasant task of explaining to members of my family why that business was not sellable. JD has spent more than 25 years as an investment banker focused on mergers and acquisitions in the middle market. His career has given me a close look at the lens through which a prospective buyer examines a prospective acquisition. A service business entirely dependent on an owner, without a product, or a client/customer list that is transferable ("sellable"), is not attractive to a prospective buyer.

When JD and I, along with our friends Preston and Lori Campbell, started Document Warehouse we had two goals. We wanted to grow a business to sell it, and we wanted to maintain our friendship. Because we shared these intentions, they became our guardrails. We agreed on the intentions and modeled every system and process after our target acquirer's ideal acquisition criteria. When the time was right, we sold Document Warehouse to our ideal buyer, Iron Mountain. Preston, Lori, JD, and I went on to start our own businesses, and the Campbells own and operate Go West Development in Park City, Utah.

In 2015, I founded Ascend Coaching Solutions which I operate from my home office in Powhatan, Virginia. Ascend is a coaching firm that specializes in working with business leaders and executives who plan to expand their leadership capacity as their responsibilities grow. Ascend offers an innovative approach to coaching at the intersection of business and life.

—Wendy Dickinson

FIDDLE WHILE YOU WORK - YOU CAN DO BOTH!

Fun Fact: Bumblebees and hawkmoths multitask. They can pivot and avoid pitfalls at the same time!

When I was a kid, every time I read or thought about Aesop's Fable "The Ants and The Grasshopper," I always felt sorry for both the ant and the grasshopper. The poor ant was a workaholic (long before we even knew what that meant), and he wasn't playing outside in the sun — which was one of our favorite things to do.

On the other hand, the poor grasshopper looks so happy playing the violin but doesn't know he is going to get crushed in a few paragraphs, along with being cold and hungry.

So, I wondered then and now, why it couldn't have been better for both of them? Why not collaborate in terms of having some fun and doing essential work? Here I am, fifty plus years later with decades of experience working with brilliant business owners. I am excited to take this wonderful fable and pass along my time-proven insights to entrepreneurs who want to be both wildly successful and happy.

For those of you who don't remember the tale, here is Aesop's Fable:

The Ants & the Grasshopper

One bright day in late autumn a family of Ants were bustling about in the warm sunshine, drying out the grain they had stored up during the summer, when a starving Grasshopper, his fiddle under his arm, came up and humbly begged for a bite to eat.

"What!" cried the Ants in surprise, "haven't you stored anything away for the winter? What in the world were you doing all last summer?"

"I didn't have time to store up any food," whined the Grasshopper; "I was so busy making music that before I knew it, the summer was gone."

The Ants shrugged their shoulders in disgust.

"Making music, were you?" they cried. "Very well; now dance!" And they turned their backs on the Grasshopper and went on with their work.

And the Moral of the Story is... *There's a time for work and a time for play.*

The moral of the story, "There's a time for work and a time for play" sounds very sensible. But business owners know, there is always work to be done. As I prepared this book for print, business owners coped with the economic fallout of COVID-19. The business landscape was in flux and the dust yet to settle. Companies agile enough to make decisive changes to their business models revised operations as needed, and survived. Those that couldn't do that, failed. Business owners know, there is always work to be done.

What is the difference between a company that is ready and with enough resilience to overcome the obstacles ahead and one that isn't? Scenario planning, solid leadership, and a willingness to adopt a growth mindset are just a few of the tools that can make the difference between creating a job for yourself and a viable company. Add in an expanded sense of self-awareness, readiness and resilience, and I believe that company becomes a valuable asset.

I'd like to set this fable up to guide you through whatever comes your way — pandemics, climate events, personal illness, or death. The better prepared you and your company are, the better your life and your business. It's a lot of work, but the return on investment can be well worth it.

That is the life of a business owner — a lot of work. Most new business owners take a 24/7 approach to growing the business. Life is out of balance, with the owner feeling a sense of urgency that overshadows their other priorities. Intellectually, owners may acknowledge that strategic planning that includes running scenarios would be a worthwhile activity, but don't see the immediate need when so many other things demand attention. As a coach, I talk with business owners who feel that this time period is a matter of "paying my dues," and that they must "make hay while the sun shines." Very much like our friend, Ant.

Business owners often create companies that reflect their skills and strengths, as well as fill a need. A lot of them have created a job for themselves. That can be enough — a steady paycheck, a sense of autonomy, and no boss. There is no end game.

These owners have created a job for themselves and not an asset to leverage market share and create wealth. The heartbreak comes in as this business owner prepares to retire. Many don't have enough in savings to retire comfortably. This reminds us of Grasshopper, doesn't it?

Years pass with a lot of owners filling many roles, wearing many hats, and missing out on opportunities with family, friends, and in their industries. One of our clients had a business for well over a decade. This person had a team, a solid client base, and did an incredible number of the day-to-day operational tasks.

Think about this. With an established business, a team, and clients, the owner was the one solving problems, onboarding new team members, and expanding services only when time opened in the owner's schedule. After ten plus years, this owner was tapped out.

This owner had no time to work ON the business — there was no ten-, five-, or three-year strategic plan or scenario planning. This owner had not consulted a financial planner, advisor, or considered what would happen to the team and the clients if the business closed or the owner was incapacitated.

It never occurred to this owner that the business could become an asset. The thought of selling their business one day was never considered. This exhausted, stressed, and grumpy owner had fallen deeply into the trap of believing that there was no other way than to be the haymaker every day and in every way.

The purpose of this business fable is to give you, the reader, the chance to take a look at your own business. You can see if your experience as a business owner is more in keeping with that of Ant's, or Grasshopper's, or a combination of the two.

Aesop and his fable, along with Ant and Grasshopper, can teach us important lessons about learning in community, discovering options, and developing a growth mindset, all of which set the business up to be ready and to build resilience. I would like to take a look at how Ant and Grasshopper could make the most out of that first meeting Aesop wrote about.

Once upon a time, at a coffee shop in the trees at the edge of the meadow, a chance meeting occurred. Ant had decided to stop by and grab a cup on his way into the fields. The family had made it through the winter — barely. Despite working hard all last summer, their supplies had run dangerously low by spring. Of course, the entire woodland community had suffered from the terrible conditions. Many barely squeaked by with the clothes on their backs. Ant realized that something had to change. He couldn't stand by and watch that happen to his family again. He had an idea that may be a long-term solution. Ant had decided to start a business.

While Ant was in line thinking thoughts of profits, year-round work, and giving all of his children an occupation outside of the fields, he was startled out of his visions by the sudden opening of the door. It flew open, the wind blowing the fresh spring air into the shop. As Ant looked up, he was amazed to see Grasshopper.

Grasshopper looked thin but was smiling. He had his scarf wound around his neck. His man-bag slung across his concave chest, papers spilling out, and the guy had an energy that drew every eye. As soon as his gaze found Ant, he started toward him.

"Hey!" Grasshopper called out. Ant was flabbergasted. The last time the two had spoken, Ant had been unkind. He had refused to help Grasshopper and thought the guy would be dead by now. Suddenly, Ant had a thought. Maybe even last fall he had known that the family's supplies weren't enough. He'd had a gut feeling things were going to get real — as in *real bad*. It was fear that drove him to be unkind. That thought filled him with shame and frustration. He did not want fear to drive his life. Yes, he would start that business, build his wealth, and hope that he could beat that kind of economic downturn if it ever happened again!

Grasshopper approached and jumped into line with Ant (ignoring the grumbling of those behind him in the line). "I just wanted to thank you. Last winter I was so angry with you for refusing to help me. I was so angry I decided to live and find a way to become rich! I'm determined to show you what I can do!"

Ant was surprised. "Well, I'm glad you survived. How do you propose to earn money? You don't seem to have any skills, or a real desire to work!"

Grasshopper replied, "I've met the love of my life. We've gotten married and plan to start a family. We are going to start a business. We have already decided on a name, Wingsong Events! After everything that happened last year in this wood, we NEED parties! I've just filed the paperwork. We're going to be rich! I will have plenty of time to play my music, enjoy married life, and my business will make the money for us! Brilliant, isn't it?"

Ant had his doubts. On the other hand, he could use some of the energy and enthusiasm that Grasshopper seems to bring wherever he goes, despite almost starving to death. After all, Ant had just made the decision NOT to live motivated by fear, right?

Ant turned his attention back to Grasshopper, who was waiting for Ant's response. "Yes, ah, that sounds like a good idea. As a matter of fact, I'm starting a business myself. I wonder, would you like to act as my accountability partner? I believe in setting up accountability for myself. It helps me stay on task, and I always need a sounding board. What do you think, would you like to be my accountability partner?"

Grasshopper's enthusiasm burst through his emphatic, "Yes! That sounds great! I think that would be good for me, too. Want to meet now?"

Ant had to refuse. "No, I have another appointment and a lot of work to do. How about we meet here tomorrow morning? Around the same time?" Ant and Grasshopper set the time and both agreed to show up tomorrow at 8:00 am.

QUIZ: ARE YOU AN ANT, A GRASSHOPPER, OR AN ANTHOPPER?

You aren't happy with the company as it is.
You:

___ Decide to just live with it
___ Decide to leave it
___ Decide to change it

Who are the 3 key people in your company?

1)
2)
3)

True or False:

___ You must build a model for leadership.
___ It is inevitable that your company will hit a plateau.
___ Change is unavoidable if you want to succeed.

____ The company needs more than one operating system (*method of running the company*) to succeed.

How important is culture to the value of your organization?

____ Very
____ Neutral
____ Who cares?

On a scale of 1 (lowest rating) to 5 (highest rating), rate your management team on the following abilities to:

____ Simplify
____ Delegate
____ Predict
____ Systemize [1]
____ Structure [2]

A 40-hour workweek converts into 160 hours of work per month. How many hours do you spend working ON your business (strategic plans, exit strategies, systems, etc.) versus IN (day-to-day operations, problem-solving, maintaining client/customer relationships) your business?

20% or less
21-40%
41% or more

State your company's value proposition and purpose.

_____
_____
_____
_____
_____
_____

How many people in the company know what that value proposition and purpose are and can communicate it to someone else?

On a scale of 1 (lowest rating) to 5 (highest rating), rate your team on adhering to each of the following:

____ Company's value proposition
____ Ideal customer experience
____ Ideal strategic partner experience
____ Ideal employee experience
____ Ideal business owner/founder experience

What are the top three values reflected in your company's culture?

1)
2)
3)

What obstacles does your company face in the next five years?

1)
2)
3)

Summary

Remember, the purpose of this tale is cautionary. We want to fill you in on what could happen, what we've seen happen, and the many ways owners have come to us for help. We hope this tale of Ant and Grasshopper will allow you to prepare to accumulate wealth, to create a successful business, and to live a meaningful life.

We want you to consider what your future may hold. Ideally, a buyer for your company will want to step into a turn-key operation. The optimal acquisition will allow the current owner to step out of leadership and the new owner to step into the leadership role without missing a beat. This means virtually no turnover, no loss in sales or customers, and from the outside, it is business as usual.

In case you have dismissed that last paragraph because you plan to pass the business off to a family member or current employee, or shut the business down, stop that story in your head right now.

That is an example of a fixed mindset. A fixed mindset can cost you money and opportunity. The goal here is for you to have as many viable options as possible when you are ready to exit. So, let's take a look at the quiz questions. We will share with you the key takeaways from each one.

You aren't happy with the company as it is.

- *List the 5 harshest facts about your company. (Facts, not opinions.)*
- *Why are these facts on the list?*
- *How does each one impact the company? How does each one impact your happiness?*
- *Why do these facts matter?*
- *What stands in the way of your happiness?*

These questions offer you the chance to look at the intersection of your life's happiness and the wellbeing of the business. The 5 harshest facts may be issues that block the company's growth and development. They may be issues that can be solved with a new perspective, approach, or shift in attitude. Use each as a lens into the wellness of the company and into your own happiness.

Who are the 3 key people in your company?

If you are one of the 3, we suggest caution. Evaluate your importance by determining the percentages of time spent in day-to-day operations, problem-solving, strategic planning, and in business development. How much of the company's revenue have you generated?

Would a new president be able to walk in tomorrow and "drive this bus"? If the answer is no, identify what needs to happen to create that kind of operation.

Are your key people happy and fulfilled?

For the others on your list, how does the company incentivize each person? What is the long-term plan for nurturing the growth and development of each person? Calculate the costs of replacing each.

Discover what each finds most rewarding and least rewarding about their work.

You must build a model for leadership.

- *Define what leadership means to you. Jim Collins, author of BE 2.0 (Beyond Entrepreneurship), defines leadership as "... the art of getting people to want to do what must be done".*
- *Find out what leadership means to the people in your organization.*
- *Compare the definitions and revise the definition of leadership accordingly.*
- *Include the different functions that keep the company alive: decision-making (delegating, consensual, participatory or autocratic), culture development (aligned with mission, vision and purpose), talent development (recruiting, retaining, and nurturing), and personal development.*

It is inevitable that your company will hit a plateau.
I think we can all agree on this one. So, prepare by getting ready for

whatever happens next. Use every chance to build the resilience in the company by building the resilience of each person in the company.

- *Hold formal and informal "what if" conversations. Post a what if question on a white board and ask everybody in the company to come by and leave a thought, suggestion, or concern. What should our first steps be if the company had to close down for a hurricane? What's our plan if we lost our biggest customer? Supplier? Get creative and see what your people come up with for each one.*
- *Pinpoint your company's weaknesses and strengths. Jim Collins frames this process in How The Mighty Fall with his 5 Stages of Decline. The 5 are: Hubris Born of Success, Undisciplined Pursuit of More, Denial of Risk & Peril, Grasping for Salvation, and Capitulation to Irrelevance or Death.*

Change is unavoidable if you want to succeed.

Your answer to this question is an indicator of mindset and awareness. A fixed mindset is costly. A growth mindset creates bandwidth for the unexpected. Culture can add value to your enterprise value, or detract from it. The mindset and level of awareness demonstrated by the president, founder, or CEO has a great deal of influence over culture.

The company needs more than one operating system (*method of running the company*) to succeed.

An operating system can mean different things — your company may have many systems for conducting business. This statement is designed to determine the level of consistency within the company. Is every person on the same page of the playbook? If not, why not?

There is no one right way to run your company. There is however, one right vision. Your operating system will evolve and change over time as your company grows and develops. The important point here is to lead

your team, their ideas and the results aligned with the vision integrated into the execution of the strategic plan.

How important is culture to the value of your organization?

Many of you have created businesses using financial models commonly used in your industry. Two opportunities to build enterprise value on the horizon are outside of the traditional financial models. One is to nurture a culture of company values with mission and purpose as guardrails that reward customers with an ideal purchasing experience and one in which employees feel rewarded with meaningful work. The other is to anticipate future innovations and disruptions to capitalize on both before your competitors.

Rate your management team on the following abilities to:

- Simplify
- Delegate
- Predict
- Systemize ("Systemizing involves clearly identifying what those core processes are and integrating them into a fully functioning machine.")
- Structure ("Your company needs to be organized in a way that reduces complexity and creates accountability. In addition, this structure should also be designed to boost you to the next level.")

This five-prong approach allows you, and your management team, to work ON your business, not just IN it. Honing in on each element in every strategic planning session allows you to begin to write the story of the company.

This story, written as it happens, sets you and the team up to present to a future buyer, or investor, a documented record of resiliency. The ups and downs are analyzed before, during, and after each event, along *with the responses. Transparency lends your company story legitimacy.*

Should you decide to sell, transparency from day one leads to a smooth due diligence. Due diligence is an opportunity for prospective buyers to uncover reasons to renegotiate the purchase price — which you definitely don't want to go through so close to your finish line.

A 40-hour workweek converts into 160 hours of work per month. How many hours do you spend working ON your business (strategic plans, exit strategies, systems, etc.) versus IN (day to day operations, problem-solving, maintaining client/customer relationships) your business?

This question is for those of you who believe and tell yourself regularly, that you do NOT have time to think about the future. We are here to tell you, using Ant and Grasshopper, that the time you spend working on your end game, your one-, three-, and five-year plans are well worth the investment.

State your company's value proposition and purpose.

Value proposition and purpose are core elements in your company story. If you have clarity around each, your ability to lead is streamlined. Both can act as guardrails in your prioritization responsibilities, problem-solving, and decision making. All essential to creating the bandwidth for self-care and strategizing, as well as establishing a legacy.

This is the place where the rubber meets the road. Your company can be a drop in the world's economy, or it can be a force for so much more than building your assets. Your choice, your company. Decide.

Build something that positively impacts your family, community, state, region and country by putting the vision out there for all to see. Build something greater than yourself, that lives and grows beyond your life. That is your legacy.

How many people in the company know what that value proposition and purpose are and can communicate it to someone else?

Once you are clear on value proposition and purpose, you can communicate both to the team. Both give guidance in determining daily, monthly, and quarterly intentions. Both provide agency for your customers' and your employees' experiences as they interact with your company's systems and processes. Remember, the clearest way to communicate vision, value proposition, and purpose is to live them in every speech, conversation, decision, and action you take.

Rate your team on adhering to each of the following:

- Company's value proposition (1 to 5)
- Ideal customer experience (1 to 5)
- Ideal strategic partner experience (1 to 5)
- Ideal employee experience (1 to 5)
- Ideal business owner/founder experience (1 to 5)

We continue to challenge you to build on the foundational building blocks of culture, values, quality customer and employee experiences, as well as purpose. The company's ability to withstand innovation and disruption can become another intangible asset.

Do a foundation checkup at every strategic planning session. SWOT (strengths, weaknesses, opportunities, and threats) assessments are particularly helpful in this type of analysis.

What are the top three values reflected in your company's culture?

Including a values assessment in your onboarding process, as well as in your team strategic planning sessions can uncover competing goals, as well as otherwise inexplicable behaviors on the part of team members. You will see that Ant and Grasshopper struggle with each other, family members, and employees when values conflict.

What obstacles does your company face in the next five years?

If you are able to answer this question, give yourself credit for utilizing foresight.

What would happen if:

You or your partner died.
There was a tornado, hurricane, or extreme drought in your area.
There was another pandemic and every person in the country was in quarantine.

This is a version of scenario planning. The keys to scenario planning are to complete both an external and internal assessment of the economy, determine your liquidity under those circumstances, then identify who on the team, board, and in the family need to be in on the decision-making. Lastly, within each scenario, determine the changes to the business model, along with any revisions to operations and set up a framework for devising a recovery plan.

If you believe that you don't have to worry about this because you are passing your company on to your kids, stop right now. This process does apply to you. Your company needs to be strong enough to stand alone without you, the founder. Your company needs to be strong enough to withstand the transition to new leadership. As a steward, your responsibility is to pass on a resilient company that can thrive without the founder.

Each of the quiz's questions are designed to stimulate thought and planning. Let's catch up with Ant and Grasshopper.

1

MAKE A MOUNTAIN OUT OF AN ANTHILL

Fun Fact: An ant can lift 20 times its own body weight.

Ant arrived at the coffee shop early. He made a habit of being early. It was disrespectful to be late. He ordered a plain, small black coffee. He would sip it slowly to make it last. Ant had devoted a lot of thought to the idea of starting a business, and getting a jump on any future disasters.

The more he thought of it, the more it seemed like starting a business was the solution to his varied needs:

- Potential for a steadier income.
- Possible positions for his family members to assume as the company grew.
- Learning opportunities for the kids to learn about business. (That last one was ironic since he needed to learn about running a business, too.)
- Potential to accumulate wealth.

The tricky part was, what kind of business should he start? He decided to make a list of his skills and interests. Ant decided to include the skills of his oldest kids. After all, he wanted to create jobs for himself and his family that could weather any kind of event. The business needed to be something that could be scaled and last long into the future. He decided to take a look at the economic growth profile of the area, too.

Ant had a couple of ideas. A commercial and residential cleaning service could offer employment opportunities for the whole family. This had growth potential since there was little competition in this area, and the startup costs would be minimal. Another plus was that it was a year-round business. The downside was that the work was uninspiring at best. Also, it could be risky during a recession, like the one last year. People tend to eliminate costs associated with luxury when times are tough.

What about a marketing company? Hmmm. Definitely more interesting work. The kids were certainly social media savvy. He and his wife were old-school with their farm and in selling their produce. They used the network of relationships started by their families years ago. They printed off their inventory to offer the most recent prices. Definitely old-school.

(Actually, his wife may want to continue running the farm — Ant added that to the list of questions to ask her.)

The overhead on a marketing business seemed high. Each of them would need to update their computers. He probably also needed training. There would be a learning curve for all of them. There were also several other marketing companies already established in the area.

No. Neither of those were right for his family.

Just then, the door of the coffee shop flew open, and Grasshopper rushed in. His man-bag was overflowing with papers, about to burst, as he moved toward Ant. Grasshopper had a big smile on his face. The energy in the room pulsed as he made his way to the table.

Ant glanced at his watch, and he realized that Grasshopper was late. It was 8:15 am. Sigh. Ant greeted Grasshopper as he wondered what he had done to suggest that they act as accountability partners for one another.

Grasshopper gushed, "Ant, I'm so glad to see you! I can't wait to get started. Wingsong Events is already off to a great start. My spouse and I love parties, music, and making that sort of magic happen. After the quarantine, and the economic implosion of last year, everyone wants to party! It's perfect for us! How about you? What have you decided to do?"

"I haven't decided yet, Grasshopper. These are the things I've thought about...," and the conversation took off from there. The two put their heads together. As the conversation progressed, both developed visions and purpose, and they took a look at values.

Grasshopper's top three values were flexibility, freedom, and abundance. Ant prioritized his top three as:

1. Family
2. Security
3. Respect

Ant's purpose for the business included accumulating wealth, providing consistently for his family, and creating the opportunity to become a respected member of the community. Grasshopper wanted to be wealthy, never starve again, and provide for his family, too.

Ant leaned forward and asked Grasshopper, "Have you thought about how Wingsong Events will withstand another pandemic? I mean, come on, we just got out of the worst economic disaster of our lifetimes." He pulled out a few sheets of paper and a bunch of sticky notes. He passed them to Grasshopper. "I found this free PDF for a business plan." Grasshopper looked surprised, but took it.

"It looks easy, and we know we both need a business plan. This is Strategyzer's Business Model Canvas Plan[1]. There are nine segments in the plan. If we use sticky notes to fill in the entries for each segment, we can move the entries around as often as we need to."

The two spent some time filling out the PDF and talking about it. Ant had decided to start an excavation business. After all, it's what ants know. As they were filling out the template, Ms. Ladybug happened to walk by their table. She stopped to take a look.

"Good Morning! What brings the two of you here today? You look very busy. I recognize the Business Model Canvas Plan." Ant and Grasshopper told her about their plans.

Grasshopper turned to Ms. Ladybug, who he remembered is the president of a successful construction business that managed to survive the downturn, and asked, "What do you think? Have any words of wisdom to lay on us?"

"I do," she said. She shared an actual list!

1. Determine your value proposition
2. Prioritize your values
3. Build strong business relationships with your customers and community
4. Hire employees to retain them
5. Build your company to eventually run without you

"If you do these five things, you will build a company that is a 'sellable asset' and not just a provider of a paycheck for you. We all know friends and neighbors who start companies that end up becoming jobs for themselves. That is totally fine, of course. My plan for *my* company, however, is to create wealth and build an asset, so that when I'm ready to exit, I will have an enterprise to sell."

Ant invited Ms. Ladybug to join them for a few minutes. She agreed. After sitting, Ant asked her to take a look at what they had come up with so far. "This looks good, guys. I'm happy to share the things I've learned and to serve as one of your mentors. You can take my advice or leave it. Use what works for you. These are things I wish someone had shared with me."

"You know that I am a home builder. We always start with a blueprint, and once the overall design is approved, we then create a set of plans that contains the specifications of each element. We can't determine particular measurements, order materials, schedule subcontractors, or choose finishes without knowing exactly what the finished product is supposed to look like. Of course, something always goes wrong. No project ever goes off exactly as planned. The thing is, we know how to generate options. We plan for problems, so we are ready when they happen. Look at me, still standing after the events of the past year."

Ms. Ladybug looked each of them in the eye as she continued. "The blueprint provides all of the people involved a clear plan for working towards a finish line. Our purpose is clearly communi-cated. We also have clarity around values — work ethic, professionalism, and accepting responsibility for our mistakes, for example. If a subcontractor's work does not meet those values (or standards), we will not work with them.

"When I started my business, I didn't bother with values, purpose, or value proposition. I decided to start my business, filled out the paperwork for my business license, visited my insurance agent to buy the right commercial policies, and started looking for my first client. From there, it was a hamster wheel. I ran from one 'fire' to another, day after day. I didn't take the time to do what you are doing today. It wasn't until I was exhausted, overwhelmed, and unable to take another day that I looked for some help." Ms. Ladybug sighed as her eyes dropped to the tabletop covered with their work and empty cups.

She looked up and smiled. "But I did get help. That led me to view the things you are doing today as necessary conversations to have day after day, year after year. Those are the things that allowed me to stay in business over the past year. There was no magic bullet, but we had a plan that we executed, then changed several times to pivot with us. But, we did it. The planning paid off way more than the plan itself. These aren't boxes to be checked off and never visited again. Your businesses will grow and evolve. Your customers will change, especially if your businesses are transactional like mine. You can hire employees to retain each one, or not. Employee development and plans to incentivize your personnel make sense in hiring to retain. It can be costly to have high employee turnover, especially in our current tight labor market."

Ms. Ladybug paused, and her gaze was steady. "Each of you has your own style. Everyone who knows you knows that about you in this community. The reputation you build with each customer becomes part of the value of your company. The people who work for you become part of the value of your company. The values, value proposition, purpose, and ideal outcomes for your customers and employees become part of the culture of the business. While they are not tangible assets like inventory or cash, those aspects of your company can add tremendous value to your company in the eyes of a buyer. I didn't know any of this when I started. Now, someone has told you, and you can decide whether to take my advice."

"Make working *on* your business as much a part of your work life as working *in* your business. Run the scenarios regularly. Build an outside board of advisors to offer multiple perspectives on your industry, to identify best practices as the business grows, and to benefit from the experiences of others to help you think through the many decisions you will have to make. I have to say, having an accountability partner seems to be a great place to start. And, if you build a relationship with me as your mentor, you then have at least two people to consult. I'd also recommend that the majority of your board consist of those outside of your family." Ms. Ladybug sat back and took a deep breath as she surveyed the room. She took a look at her watch and seemed to prepare to rise, then settled back again. Ms. Ladybug looked at them and held up one leg.

Her serious gaze settled on Ant and then Grasshopper in turn. "The one thing I'd encourage you to do today is to spend fifteen minutes thinking about your exit strategy. That's the only thing I believe you are missing."

Grasshopper was stunned. "I had no idea there were so many things to think about like that. I really thought I could just click through this list because we have already started Wingsong. Who knew?" He turned to Ant and was startled. Grasshopper thought Ant was so much further along in all of this than he was. After all, Ant always looked totally in control and appeared confident to the point of arrogance. But, right now, Ant appeared annoyed.

Grasshopper looked at Ant who was shaking his head. "So, Ant, what do you think? You look like you just shut down. What just happened?"

Ant, shaking his head, replied, "I don't understand why I need to think about exiting when I've just made a decision about what kind of business I'm going to start. I think my time and energy are better spent on getting my business license, my first customers, and my office set up. After all, look at how many businesses failed as a result of the pandemic. This seems like I'd be getting ahead of myself."

Ms. Ladybug leaned in to respond. "You aren't alone in feeling that way, Ant. However, I've learned from my mentors, board, attorney, and accountant that creating scenario plans and an exit plan were as important steps as the first step that I missed. That hurt my bottom line. Now my scenario planning and exit strategy inform many of the decisions I make in my business every day. The options that my exit strategy has generated for me over the years are valuable to me. I would encourage the two of you to do the same. Start today with fifteen minutes to envision your ideal exit. Make it as detailed as possible. Revisit it from time to time, too. Make that exit strategy a living part of your company's culture. Then, when you have several hours to give to it, run scenarios like the one we just lived through.

"And, you know, part of that ongoing work to bring your exit strategy to life is to develop relationships with advisors who can support your plan as you grow your company. Don't wait to engage an attorney and an accountant. Seek out a financial planner to take a look at what your business needs to generate to allow you to retire."

She continued, "I'd be happy to be a mentor for both of you. There are so many things I regret. But, I have to go now. Let me know if you'd like to set something up to meet regularly as mentor and mentees." Ms. Ladybug smiled warmly.

Both Ant and Grasshopper looked thoughtful and thanked Ms. Ladybug for her insights and her offer. Ms. Ladybug pushed back from the table and left.

And the Moral of the Story is... *Dream big but sweat the small stuff.*

The advice that Ms. Ladybug gave to Ant and Grasshopper in this meeting is often overlooked and undervalued by most founders. Many work very hard in their companies with an eye to making a profit next quarter and by year's end, but few give thought to the experiences their customers and employees will have, the future opportunities and threats of the company, and to their retirement. Those things seem far away, at least in the very beginning.

The Strategyzer Business Model Canvas Plan for business plans is one that we have used and that our clients and students find useful. It has nine components:

1. Customer segments
2. Value proposition
3. Channels — communication, distribution, and sales
4. Customer relationships within each segment
5. Revenue streams
6. Key resources
7. Key activities
8. Key partnerships — activities that are outsourced
9. Cost structure

One of our clients looked for a business coach because her brick-and-mortar business was failing. She had owned and operated the business for a number of years, and she had reached the point that Ms. Ladybug described — exhausted, overwhelmed, and losing money. This client knew she needed help and sought it out. By taking the time to work on her business — assessing her values, purpose, ideal outcomes, and the experience that she wanted to have as a business owner, as well as the experiences she'd like to be able to deliver to her customers and employees — she was able to gain a great deal of clarity. Here is what she discovered:

- The hours of operation were not sustainable with her current staff
- The business was not consistently profitable
- Overhead was a significant factor in failing to turn a profit
- The brick-and-mortar building was not vital to the core purpose or value proposition
- There were several sources of undeveloped, but consistent, revenue
- She needed to consider developing an online model for the business

The Business Model Canvas Plan allowed this client to play with possibilities that included a new online business. As this idea took shape, the client created a business without inventory, overhead, or the time needed to maintain and manage a physical location. The idea continues to serve her targeted client segment, the value proposition is still relevant, and her key partnerships remain strong.

This new enterprise aligns with her values and purpose, and it increases the chances of her achieving an ideal exit strategy. Using the Business Model Canvas Plan as a tool within the coaching relationship acted as inspiration. This client designed her business to align with her desired business owner experience, or B(O)x for short. Her B(O)x allowed her to summarize her customer experience and strategic partnerships on one page, enabling her to be mindful of her ultimate goals during meetings.

Planning for your future exit is a worthwhile and critically important investment of your time and energy. Why? Because creating an exit strategy from day one will allow you to avoid the problems that will make your business difficult to sell or create a lasting legacy for family members to take over the business in the future.

Here are a few statistics on this topic that you may find interesting:

1. Just 18% of family businesses have a robust succession plan (one of which could be a
2. sale). Twenty-seven percent have no plans at all. This is a recipe for disaster — assumptions, interpretations, misplaced beliefs, and expectations wreak havoc on family relationships.
3. Family governance is the process of formalizing family decisions. These are decisions that happens both in formal meetings and on an informal, need based, decisions that happen in the moment and turn out to be good ones for the long term as well.
4. Informal governance is going to be a success in today's economy and more difficult for family businesses. ~Jonathan Flack, US Family Business Leader
5. Seventy percent of business partnerships ultimately fail.
6. Relationships affect your customers, too. Esteban Kolsky found that 13% of unhappy customers will share their complaints with fifteen people. Only one customer in twenty-five will tell the owner about the complaint. And, for customers who don't complain, they just don't come back. If the relationship between you and your employees isn't harmonious, it matters. Your customers will notice.
7. Seventy-five to ninety percent of businesses that launch a sale process ultimately are not sold. How can business owners prepare for this possibility?
8. Of the approximately 25% that do sell, 75 – 90% of those are considered a failure, often due to failing to integrate successfully. What steps can owners take to build strong cultures of readiness, resilience, and legacy?
9. Take a look at Bain & Co.'s Value Pyramid. There are two versions: a B2B and B2C. There is also a values assessment for you to use to determine your values at the end of this chapter.

Many business owners allow the company to revolve around them, either consciously or unconsciously. That type of owner is often heavily involved in the day-to-day operations. They problem-solve, have the final say on new initiatives, and are reluctant to take vacations because they fear what might happen when they are away. (By the way, if you are one of those owners who do go on vacation, but are on the phone with the company constantly, then you fall into this category as well!)

These owners fail to design systems and processes that serve the company's growth and development. They fail to empower their leadership team to generate new projects and to solve their own problems. The challenge with this type of business is that a new owner cannot see themselves as able to step into the role of the owner without a potentially painful and prolonged transition. Your job, therefore, is to build your company to stand on its own.

Founding a company is an opportunity to create an independent entity with its own story, identity, and purpose. This company has its own value proposition, strengths, and weaknesses. Each company has its own possibilities, too.

To prepare a company for a sale, the company story, culture, and management team are as important as the income statement and balance sheet. A great example of a successful exit strategy in which culture played a significant role is Janet Kraus' company, Circles, which was sold in 2007[2]. As Janet told this story in Dallas in July 2019, we were amazed to learn that Circles sold at seventeen times the earnings before interest, taxes, depreciation, and amortization (EBITDA) due to the people inspired by the culture of the business. That was an amazing accomplishment.

Business owners with companies that are of little value to prospective buyers are far more common than you might think. And the fact is that most business owners plan to fund at least some part of their retirement through the successful sale of their company. Obviously, this is a huge problem for those who have, unknowingly, fallen into one of the all-too-common pitfalls of creating an "unsellable" company. We want to be crystal clear here. If you have created a job for yourself, so be it. However, chances are that sort of business won't be of much value to a potential buyer or investor, and chances are it won't withstand a major economic catastrophe.

Another common problem can be an owner's "grandiose, inflated valuation expectations," which we call the GIVE Syndrome. Ultimately, your company is worth what a willing buyer will pay for it, versus what you think it's worth, or how much you need to live on for retirement. As a business owner, therefore, one important thing you can do is to follow best practices for accounting, which will enable you (with outside help) to determine a fair market value for your business before approaching buyers.

If you set your company up, from day one, with comprehensive accounting and bookkeeping practices, you will be able to provide the necessary documentation to your external advisors to accurately assess the value of your company when you are ready to exit. Of course, that assumes you've planned ahead by engaging a reputable outside accounting firm, and when the time was right, hired a strong bookkeeper or controller to track your business' financial performance accurately and consistently over the course of the company's history.

So, as a next step, take a look at Strategyzer's Business Canvas Model. Has your business changed? What is your exit strategy? What does that next chapter look like for you? Will your company be ready to transition successfully? Will your management team be prepared?

That, friends, is your goal. The more options you have when you are ready to exit your business, the more opportunities you have to exit <u>successfully</u>. We encourage you to establish practices through which you can generate as many viable options as possible so that no matter what life has in store for you, you are ready. Demonstrated resilience goes hand in hand with readiness. The ups and downs of your industry, markets, and company performance can be vital parts of the story that you present to prospective buyers and investors, as well as your outside advisors.

Start with the Business Canvas Model that is found at the end of this chapter. Play with the Future Foundation. Ask your team to do the same. Build a company that reflects your ideal B(O)x, from day one to the last day. Your company, on your terms.

Use the Business Model Canvas as your one-page business plan. You can either write this in your journal, or visit Strategyzer's website at www.ascendcoachingsolutions.com for the form template. Please refer to Strategyzer's website for additional instructions.

The Business Model Canvas

Key Partners	Key Activities	Value Propositions	Customer Relationships	Customer Segments
	Key Resources		Channels	

Cost Structure		Revenue Streams	

Designed for: Designed by: Date: Version:

Strategyzer

strategyzer.com

Use the Future Foundation to chart your company's future growth and development. You can either write this in your journal or visit our website at www.ascendcoachingsolutions.com for the form template. Measure each new initiative against your company's values. Once you have identified your company's top four values, capture them. Revisit the value proposition you identified using Strategyzer's Business Model Canvas Plan and capture it. Next, identify key customers and future strategic partners, innovations that could lead to increased market share, and opportunities to step out of the day-to-day operations as much as possible.

We suggest that you revisit these activities every three to six months. Your goal is to design the systems and processes for customer acquisition to align with your values and exit strategy. You can actively seek out innovations to determine the impact on the company's longevity. Consider the return on investment as you explore ways to empower your management team and allow you, the CEO, to step out of the day-to-day operations (when the time is right) and focus on growing the company.

Many owners find it tricky to figure out when the time is right. Let's borrow the Balanced Scorecard concept from Art Schneiderman and reconfigure it for our purposes. Let's say that your financial outcomes depend on the successful execution of strategies for operations, customer sales, and your team, multiplied by you (the owner as leader and holder of the company vision). Measure each of these sectors. When one has reached or surpassed your projections, use this as a signal to consider stepping out of the lead role in this area and off board it to a new hire or a current team member. Reach out to a mentor or your informal board to determine what is a reasonable action. It may be that profits have climbed, sales are high and the two areas have surpassed forecasts. You could decide to hire a sales representative and a fractional

CFO/Bookkeeper. Either leaves you, the owner, with the influence of a multiplier on each area, but frees you to work on operations and strategy.

FUTURE FOUNDATION

Align each of your Top 4 Values with your growth strategies:

Align the company's Value Proposition with values & strategies:

Identify key customers & future strategic partners:

Identify Innovations that could lead to increased marketshare:

What are the opportunities to step out of the day to day operations:

ASCEND COACHING SOLUTIONS

2

BUILD YOUR COLONY AND DESIGN YOUR CLOUD

Fun Fact: A group of ants is a colony, and a group of grasshoppers is called a cloud!

Ant arrived early and walked into the coffee shop with his briefcase, whiteboard, a sense of excitement, and a bounce in his step. He found a table with three chairs, he looked around for some sign of Grasshopper, and he got in line for coffee.

The line moved slowly, but Ant's thoughts were anything but slow. He had decided to accept Ms. Ladybug's offer to mentor him. He had also decided on the excavation business. Goodness knows, the family had plenty of experience in site preparation and earth moving! The kids loved the idea. And, since his wife did not want to be highly involved in the day-to-day operations of their business, Ant felt comfortable with his abilities to build an excavation business without her full-time participation.

Ant hoped to persuade Grasshopper to accept Ms. Ladybug's mentorship, too. Ant believed it would help both of them to have the perspective of an experienced businesswoman like Ms. Ladybug.

Ant had met with Ms. Ladybug two weeks prior, and it was an illuminating experience. He had continued to struggle to reconcile the many things that needed to be done based on Ms. Ladybug's advice on planning for his exit strategy. Ant prided himself on being logical. He didn't believe in wasting time on dreaming big dreams when there was work to be done. Given the economic punch the past twelve months had delivered to the entire community, scenario planning he totally understood. It was that practice that allowed his family to survive the winters. Many thought summer was just a time for play, but Ant knew that summer was really the time for work.

Imagine his surprise when Ms. Ladybug outlined her business' growth and development story. She allowed him to take a look at her numbers before she had an exit strategy, as well as after the strategy was developed. The decisions that her team made, and the priorities they set at that time, were very different before pulling together a viable exit strategy.

Ms. Ladybug also shared that she and her team didn't make time for scenario planning. She had laughed and shrugged while confessing that her philosophy had been, "Why look for trouble?" Ms. Ladybug then expressed her gratitude that not only was the exit planning done before the pandemic, but so was the scenario planning. Her team had been ready for a disaster. They had not planned for that particular disaster but they had stored personal protective gear (thinking about flooding and mold), masks, and disposable coveralls on hand.

They were also certified for disaster mitigation with the ability to do duct cleaning and mold remediation, and those had allowed them to serve business owners in the community beyond the shutdown as they were considered essential personnel. This forward-thinking saved them during the pandemic. Ant understood this and thought it was a sound practice. It was the exit strategy that seemed unnecessary, until he talked with Ms. Ladybug.

Before designing her exit plan, Ms. Ladybug had simply consulted an attorney to incorporate and draft a contract for the work she did for clients, but that was it. She wore as many hats as possible in the company for as long as possible. She was the forewoman, project manager, HR department, logistics supervisor, bookkeeper, and anything else that she could do herself to save money and to be "efficient."

Amazingly, Ms. Ladybug was able to sustain this pace for almost five years. As the fifth anniversary approached, however, she hit a wall. Ms. Ladybug's health, her personal life, and her company were all in poor shape. She needed to make a change, but she didn't know what that change should look like. Ms. Ladybug decided that the first order of business was a vacation to clear her mind and get a different perspective on the situation.

So, Ms. Ladybug closed down the company for one week. She realized quickly that there was no one who could do all of the jobs that she did herself, and she had not invested in or developed her team. No one could step in while Ms. Ladybug was on vacation. The entire company revolved around her abilities and decision-making. That was a wakeup call. Ms. Ladybug knew that had to change if she wanted her company to be scalable and sustainable or if she wanted to simply survive herself. Therefore, the first decision that Ms. Ladybug made was to announce to everyone in the company that work would cease on the following Friday at 5:00 pm and would resume in ten days, beginning with a company-wide meeting at 8:00 am sharp.

The "off" week flew by with part of each day set aside for creating a 1-, 3-, and 5-year plan, scenario planning, and her ideal exit strategy, as well as a self-care plan. Ms. Ladybug met with an accountant, a business coach, and her attorney. Her attorney and the accountant recommended a couple of financial planners. Both pointed out that Ms. Ladybug needed to know what her financial goals were to accurately gauge the viability of a future sale of her company.

Equally important, Ms. Ladybug hired a business coach to work with her to develop an authentic leadership style, versus her "go-to" command-and-control style. As she and her coach worked together, important themes emerged. One such theme was a belief that didn't serve the company or Ms. Ladybug as a leader. Ms. Ladybug discovered that often she didn't believe that she was enough – not good enough or smart enough to lead a profitable company. As a result, she often did things herself to save money that needed to be assigned to a member of her management team. The team felt as though she was micromanaging strategy execution and undermining their abilities. This belief created the untenable pattern of little to no self-care, an absence of systems and processes, and an underutilized, underdeveloped group of employees.

While the week brought to light issues that Ms. Ladybug had pushed aside for years, she also seized it for the opportunity that it was. She worked with her coach to establish her guardrails and prioritize her values, including:

1. Professionalism
2. Accomplishment

3. Financial Security

In addition, she mapped out her exit strategy. Ms. Ladybug was determined to grow her company to a level of at least $2.5 million in sales. Moreover, she wanted to build relationships with at least ten strategic partners every year. Ideally, as she grew her company, she wanted to establish strategic partnerships with commercial builders in the area. Specifically, she wanted commercial builders that may become referral sources, prospective buyers, and allow for labor sharing. The idea of strategic partnerships would not have occurred to Ms. Ladybug before meeting with her coach. She also outlined a marketing strategy consisting of testimonials, videos, and social media reviews that highlighted her many satisfied clients.

Ms. Ladybug's goal was ultimately to sell her company to a private equity group or a strategic buyer. She committed to weighing each of her decisions using her exit strategy, analysis of industry trends, and her values as guardrails to determine how to allocate resources.

Ms. Ladybug achieved her goals within three years. She shared with Ant that a large part of the success was due to the development of her management team. Each person set learning and experience goals that aligned with their personal ambitions within the company. Each person had a voice at the table during the annual strategic planning process, which included scenario planning. Each person also celebrated the victories and learned from the disappointments.

Ms. Ladybug was clear with Ant that the work she did to get to this place in the company's history was hard. And, she presented a case for including scenario and exit planning regularly. Ms. Ladybug attributed both to her company's ability to survive the pandemic. While she spent many hours with her advisors and her team to achieve those goals, she was adamant that it was worth every minute and dollar invested.

As Ant reflected on everything that Ms. Ladybug had presented, he realized that developing an exit strategy upfront did, in fact, make a lot of sense. He needed to come up with a basic, but clear, goal for a desired outcome. With that decision made, he looked up and realized it was his turn to order. Just then, Grasshopper walked in, and he rushed over to buy some coffee.

Grasshopper offered a cheery hello, and Ant indicated the table he had chosen. They both walked over and sat. Grasshopper leaned in and confided, "Things are off to a great start! Wingsong has signed up three client events since we last met. I've had everyone put down a deposit, and I've downloaded contracts from our favorite online legal minds. It's been so much fun meeting with vendors, as well as prospective clients. How about you, Ant? How are things with your business?"

Talking with Grasshopper always felt overwhelming to Ant, so he leaned back to answer. "I've started an excavation and site preparation business. It's something that my kids and I have done on an informal basis in the greater Antville community for years. I've spent the past month generating relationships with builders, both commercial and residential. I've also gotten commercial insurance, started the paperwork with the SBA to fund equipment leases, and met with my attorney to draft a customer contract template. I have an appointment to begin working with a financial planner on what my wife and I need to retire comfortably. And, finally, I have selected a part-time controller to handle invoicing, payables, and all of the bookkeeping. It's been a busy month!"

Grasshopper looked curious as he asked, "Do you have any customers yet? How did you decide to meet with those people before you had any customers? I don't get it."

It was Ant's turn to lean in. "Grasshopper, I spent several hours with Ms. Ladybug after our last meeting. She started her company eight years ago. You remember that offer to mentor us, right? I believe both of us should take her up on her offer because she has so much helpful experience. I couldn't believe that her company had so many ups and downs. And, her company not only survived the last economic disaster, they actually made money."

As Grasshopper thought about what Ant was doing, versus what he was doing, he became slightly anxious. He sighed, "What kinds of ups and downs? And I still don't understand why you are meeting with all of these people. You are spending money you don't have yet. That can't be a good idea."

Ant answered with confidence. "You are right. I don't have customers yet. However, when I get my first customer, I will have everything in place to handle each with professionalism and efficiency. I don't just want a job — I want Ant Hill Excavation to become an asset for my family that will fund my retirement."

He continued, "Remember, after our last meeting here, I was stuck on why I should spend time and money on an exit strategy. Now, I get it. Ms. Ladybug walked me through her decision-making process, both before she had an exit strategy and then after. The impact on her ability to make good decisions, to build her management team, and to have a real personal life was unmistakable. I am going to start this business so that I don't have to live in constant fear that my family won't have enough to make it through the winter or anything else that comes up. I plan to do everything I can to accumulate wealth, contribute to our community, and create a legacy for future generations."

Grasshopper shook his head. "You know, I think you're right. I'd like for Ms. Ladybug to mentor me, too. I hope she can be as helpful to me as she seems to be for you. Our businesses are totally different, and I think we're going to be very different business owners. I mention those two things only to point out the benefits of differences, as well as the challenge to help one another despite the differences.

"What about employees? I have already hired my first salesperson, Cricket. Cricket landed those three customers I mentioned. Of course, now I am running a deficit instead of a profit. But, from what I understand, you have to do that sometimes. I feel a whole lot better about it now that I know you are spending before you've generated any revenue. By the way, would you mind picking up the tab for our coffee? I'm a bit short on cash." Grasshopper shifted his gaze away and then back to Ant.

"Of course, Grasshopper. But next time you pick up my tab." Ant sighed. He doubted that Grasshopper would ever pick up the tab. "I'm glad to hear that you are willing to have Ms. Ladybug mentor you. I asked her to stop by again today. Also, I believe we need to meet once a week. I just don't know that we will stay on track if we only meet monthly.

"About those differences you mentioned. You've given me a lot to think about. Let me ask you this — who will take care of project management and your books? It looks to me like you've gotten ahead of yourself." Ant continued, "It seems fun to visit venues, meet with vendors, and play music. But, what I don't hear you talking about are the systems and processes you've put into place to have your wedding reception and other "big event" customers really enjoy working with you. I think your business will rely at least initially on word-of-mouth referrals. How will you leverage goodwill once you've created it? We both have a lot of questions. Hopefully, Ms. Ladybug can help us answer them."

Nodding, Grasshopper reached for his bag and pulled out his portable tablet. "Let's get started. What's first?" The two spent the next hour looking at their business plans and discussing what systems needed to be in place for customers. The time flew by. Before they knew it, Ms. Ladybug pulled up a chair and greeted them.

Grasshopper stood and said, "Ms. Ladybug, if the offer still stands, I'd like for you to mentor me, too. Ant briefed me. I've already learned a lot and want to learn whatever you can teach me. Thank you for your offer! Ant and I have decided to meet once a week from now on. Could we meet with you that often, too?"

Ms. Ladybug smiled, "Grasshopper, I'd be happy to do it. I want to spare anybody else the mistakes that I made over those first five years. It makes total sense for the two of you to meet every week. But I'd like to meet with the two of you once a month for an hour, not every week. It will save a lot of time if you email questions that you have before we meet so that we can discuss whatever is most important to you. We can cover a lot of ground in that hour if we are prepared."

Both Ant and Grasshopper agreed. As Ms. Ladybug placed her laptop on the table, she said, "Let's get started." Each listened closely as Ms. Ladybug told her company story. She asked to see the work that both had completed based on the Business Model Canvas plan, their values assessments, and their preliminary exit strategies. Ant discussed setting up the business to pass on to his children. His exit strategy was a succession plan. Grasshopper's exit strategy was to sell the business to the highest bidder when he was ready to retire.

The hour ended with an action plan for both new business owners. The three set up their next meeting. Then, Ms. Ladybug left. Ant and Grasshopper looked at one another, nodded, and set up their meeting for the following week. Their time together had been time well spent!

And the Moral of the Story is... *The team makes the dream!*

Thirty percent of new businesses fail within the first two years. Fifty percent fail within five years. Sixty-six percent fail in ten years. The bottom line is that only 25% make it to fifteen years.[1]

Tony Robbins gets at the "why" of these sobering statistics when he identified the following challenges for new business owners in his article entitled, "5 Pain Points of a Growing Business":[2]

1. Process or systems problems
2. Innovation problems
3. Cultural problems
4. Lack of capital

5. Marketing problems

In my experience, this list is very typical. You can find a version of it almost anywhere, so we would like to spend the rest of this chapter by sharing our thoughts on these five key observations. For starters, consider the decisions that Ant and Grasshopper have made to this point. Ant identified Grasshopper's lack of attention to systems and processes. One of my clients struggled with this one. Let's call him Stuart. He had a twelve-year-old business on the cusp of another growth spurt. To that point, Stuart had saved money by doing everything he could himself. Stuart did not have a process for delegating responsibilities to the appropriate team members as the business grew. The growth happened, but Stuart was not prepared.

In order for Stuart to grow the business in a sustainable manner, he needed to promote someone to a full-time operations VP role, while he focused his attention on strategy and growth as CEO. We called this process shifting from a managerial mentality to a *CEO mindset*. Over several months, Stuart worked to distance himself from the minutiae associated with operations. He focused instead on (i) developing his VP using assessments for values, skills, and cognitive abilities, (ii) VP-level learning and experience goals designed to bring the person's strengths into alignment with the position, and (iii) developing an onboarding process for those who hold the VP position in the future.

Stuart created additional buy-in from the VP candidate by including the person in the development process, then revisiting the company's purpose and mission. Stuart was delighted to find that this change increased his capacity as CEO while creating exciting opportunities for the new VP. This was a big win for both of them, the VP was excited about the future and it set Stuart up to sell his company when the time was right.

Importantly, prospective buyers also value companies that are able to respond successfully to innovation. We live in a world of exponential change. There are many examples of companies that failed once management chose to "stay the course" with traditional business models and strategies, rather than adapt and innovate. Kodak, Blackberry, Nokia, and Blockbuster are a few that come to mind. While Ant and Grasshopper currently appear to be safe from innovation in their respective businesses, change is very hard to predict, so they have to be ready.

While some companies fail to keep up with innovation, others struggle to retain talented employees as the changes occur. This is where culture plays such an important role in generating profit. Like many business owners, Grasshopper has not given the elements of culture much thought. However, if he creates a culture of loyalty, community, and fun, his employees will respond to that vibe. They will feel like a part of an evolving team, with less turnover which is a cost savings.

A strong culture based on values, mission, and purpose often results in low employee turnover. This, too, is of value to a prospective buyer. Grasshopper plans to sell his business "when the time is right." If Grasshopper can develop a profitable business with a portfolio of successful events, glowing customer testimonials, and a team of loyal, fun, community-minded people, he has significantly increased his chances of selling his business.

Ant needs to keep these elements of a successful business in mind, too. In order to successfully transition Ant Hill Excavation to his children, he will want to develop a company with steady revenue growth, sound systems and processes, be ready for innovation, and develop a strong culture to drive sustainable growth and value.

It's too early in the story of their companies for us to assess how Ant and Grasshopper will handle innovation and develop their culture. At this point, Ant plans to employ his children, and Grasshopper has hired Cricket to lead the sales efforts. While we don't yet know the impact of those decisions, we will see the results later in the fable.

Let's turn our attention next to the capital needs of a business. Ant has equipment rentals, insurance to buy, and a bookkeeper to pay. To fund these expenditures, Ant plans to secure financing through the Small Business Administration (SBA). His friend, Grasshopper, has yet to begin to work through the issues associated with the capital needs of his company, which already has an employee on the payroll. Neither has discussed employee benefits, insurance for equipment and/or errors and omissions liability, or overhead.

Another topic that Ant and Grasshopper have yet to address is research in their respective industries. Industry data can be essential in developing an effective business plan. It can also be helpful to conduct interviews with prospective customers, as well as gather information on competitors and strategic partners. It would be interesting to include questions to paint the picture of these businesses before and then after the pandemic.

So, let's see what Ant and Grasshopper encounter in the next chapter of our fable.

Use the Value Equation to identify factors that are working against creating value, as well as components that set up your company to be an asset. There may be investments you've made in your business, and it may not be clear yet whether it will be a wasted cost. List these under Mixed/Neutral. Feel free to make lists in your journal or you can visit www.ascendcoachingsolutions.com website and download the PDF.

The goal for using this equation is to identify options that serve the company with short-term gains as well as long-term value. It is so easy to lose sight of the long-term value when it is easier or saves time to get something done in the short term. Use this in your scenario planning, too. Keep this close at hand while you go to the next activity.

Use the Life Events Timeline to map the events in your personal life that will impact your ability to be fully present in your business. Weddings, graduations, retirements, vacations, commemorative events — these are just a few of the events that can distract owners from the business. Determine what your interests are, and when you plan to begin to devote time to those interests on the Life Events Timeline. Feel free to make the list in your journal or you can visit www.ascendcoachingsolutions.com website and download the PDF.

Compare and combine the two tools. If there are factors working against creating value in the business, take a look at your timeline. How much time do you have to change that factor from a detractor to value-added? What do you need to succeed? When might be the optimal time to try? Apply this same inquiry process to the Mixed/Neutral items. For those that are value-added, what needs to happen to keep that component in the value side of the equation? How can the company maintain the status of that component?

Identify your timeline for retirement and define what retirement means for you. What needs to happen in your business before the company is of the greatest monetary value? How prepared are you for a successful retirement? The goal for using these tools is to give you, the owner, the opportunity to take manageable action steps towards your desired exit. Work to create wealth in your business. Work to create a sustainable legacy. Build a better business AND a better life.

Here are a few examples of how clients have used the Value Equation chart to determine possible ways to build value in the business, as well as identify those that have little or no value added. One client noticed that membership sales had dropped. The owner decided, without consulting the team, to offer a discounted membership with a marketing campaign to support the sale. While the short term gain of increased membership holds appeal, the longer term impact was not a value add. Here's why: other members could resent the decrease and decided not to renew at the full price and the discounted members may disproportionately take up space in the classes. This owner had lost sight of the operations costs in the costs of goods/services sold. Discounted memberships would not be value added to the long term revenue generation or to the owner's intention to franchise. As a result, this is an example of an initiative that would be placed on the left hand, factors working against creating value end of the Value Equation line. Note the costs and possible impacts of the initiative, too.

In another example, a company contemplated a new product line. The product would complement the current product lines offered and could provide a new entry point for those products. The owners had the capacity and capabilities to bring on this product line. This new product line would require additional training for the sales team. Often sales representatives are reluctant to sell new products until they see the benefit. Using the Value Equation, the owners decided to proceed with the new product line building in cost of training as well as dedicated space for the new product line materials and fabrication. This new product line could be an asset in building value in the company. So, this one would be placed on the right end of the equation line, with the costs and revenue projections noted.

V A L U E

e q u a t i o n

Factors working against creating value in your business

Mixed/Neutral aspects of the internal & external business landscape

Components that set your company up to be an asset in the eyes of prospective buyer

www.ascendcoachingsolutions.com

You may wonder how the events in your personal life play a role in the Value Equation. Let me give you a recent example. I have a client who has had two businesses for several years. One was to be sold at the "right time" and the other was to be the passion project. This client does not intend to retire and sit in a recliner. The vision is to grow the passion business. Over the past year COVID had a negative impact on sales, revenue, and the team demanded more of the owner's energy to manage while working remotely. Simultaneously, the owner's health and well-being deteriorated during the same time period. Efforts to outsource were measured using the Value Equation. Each configuration led to the conclusion that while some could be value added, none offered the client the immediate relief of the day to day operations that drained the owner's energy both physically and mentally. The owner also discovered that a new grandchild was on the way which brought to mind visions of holding that child, while taking an active part in his or her life. Ultimately, the client decided to close the business. This meant an initial outlay of energy in vetting a new service provider for clients to continue receiving services. However, within six to eight weeks, the client was able to focus on the passion project and the new life about to enter the family. Life and business do intersect. It requires navigation using values, purpose and an overarching view of both the events in life and the business.

LIFE EVENTS

timeline

Past significant events

Future significant events

Best/Worst of Today

www.ascendcoachingsolutions.com

One client has decided to retire by going part-time in the business in the next 3-5 years. His children, ages 25 and 26, may not be ready to assume ownership of the business. At this point in their careers, they are in the midst of building their leadership skills and learning the business. This owner knew that in order for his time-line to work, he needed to bring in help to prepare the next generation for leadership and to make an informed decision about ownership of the company. As a result, he considered a range of options – selling outright, selling to the younger generation, or selling a minority interest to a private equity group to allow the company to grow while the "kids" decide on fit within the company. At the same time, this client may choose to bring in a new product line within the next 3 years. That option is under consideration by management. However, the owner's timeline for retirement plays an important role in the value of the company and in the decision to expand the product offerings.

3

CHOOSE TO BE THE WINDSHIELD, NOT THE BUG

Fun Fact: The honeybee is capable of carrying its own bodyweight in pollen and nectar. It is able to fly when fully loaded!

The next week, Ant arrived at their normal location a few minutes early, and he took a quick look around. He spotted an empty table near the back and started walking toward it. Ant glanced at each of the customers, but no Grasshopper. While that didn't surprise him, it was a little disappointing.

Ant dropped his bag in a chair and put the small whiteboard on the table. He then made his way to the line, chatting with neighbors while he waited to order. When it was his turn, he debated ordering for Grasshopper, too. He decided against it. Ant had an odd feeling that Grasshopper might not show up for some reason.

Over the past year, the two had forged a working relationship that proved helpful, much to Ant's surprise. He was willing at this point to admit that going into the accountability relationship, Ant assumed he would be helping Grasshopper. He had not expected how much he would learn from his green buddy.

Grasshopper's energy was contagious. He approached networking with a level of enthusiasm that Ant admired. It wasn't just the guy's easygoing manner — Ant also admired Grasshopper's ability to forge real connections with "hard-nosed" vendors, who referred him to their customers. Grasshopper valued his clients, too. He approached each with a sincere desire to deliver the very best service. Wingsong Events represented fun, beautiful experiences, so his clients were really happy with Grasshopper and his team.

Grasshopper was also generous in introducing Ant to his contacts, and he had stepped up to endorse Ant to his clients and his network. As a result, Ant had obtained new business through Grasshopper. Ant attributed quite a bit of incremental revenue to the accountability relationship. Ant, too, had gotten comfortable with Grasshopper's professionalism and delivery of services. Ant knew that Grasshopper was a stickler for the details of every customer experience. Ant admired Grasshopper, who took a personal interest in making sure each event was as close to perfect as possible.

A few months back, Ant had realized that Grasshopper might be headed for one of the pitfalls that Ms. Ladybug had run into during her first five years of business. She had cautioned both of them about this one. She called it the BIMBO syndrome, which stands for the "Business Is My Baby Owner." Ant took this advice to heart, knowing that this was the kind of trap someone like him could easily fall into.

Ant had learned that he used what is commonly referred to as a "fixed mindset." He thought he knew himself and his kids well enough that he didn't need to ask for help or to listen to new ideas. Ant was a perfectionist, and he could get lost in the details. This slowed down their projects, and in the beginning, created inefficiencies that cost the company money. Ms. Ladybug recommended hiring a business coach, as she had had great success with one.

So, always the student, Ant looked into it. He interviewed Ms. Ladybug's coach and a few others. The one Ms. Ladybug used, Ms. Bee, specialized in family businesses, so he hired her. Ms. Bee helped Ant and his kids work through their communication issues. They worked to build a business relationship based on an expanded sense of awareness, readiness, and resilience. They saw positive impacts on their relationships within the family, too. When Ant's wife sourced several leads for projects through her contacts, Ant was equipped to express the gratitude he felt for his wife, as well as his wounded pride in having to "depend" on others for the success of the business.

The coach helped Ant and his family define their roles within the company, as well as identify what each person brought to the role. They communicated as a team, working through the progression and expectations of Ant's ultimate succession plan. They agreed on KPI's (key performance indicators) for their development, which included learning and experience goals that each would need to achieve before any promotion or increase in compensation. They also worked with an exit strategist to begin to explore ways for the employed family members to invest in the company, as well as how to compensate those who would not hold an operating role at the company.

Ant also employed radical transparency on the advice of his business coach. The resulting clarity of expectations, and the ascension of several of the kids within the ranks of the company and the family, meant that Ant gained an unexpected level of confidence in his kids. They developed a process for debriefing after the completion of every project. They looked at what went well, along with the glitches and the breakdowns in communication, as well as the opportunities to learn from every job. It was invaluable and helped the company improve and grow their profit margins.

Consulting an estate planner was another step that Ant had chosen to take. His attorney had recommended that Ant and his wife work on their wills, succession plans, and a valuation of the business to determine adequate insurance coverage. At first, Ant balked. This seemed to be getting way ahead of things, and it cost a lot of money! But, after listening to the attorney's horror stories about owners who died unexpectedly without these items in place, Ant knew he wouldn't rest easy until they were done. The attorney also cautioned Ant about treating this like a "one and done" type of task. These topics would need to be addressed on a regular basis as part of an annual strategic planning process.

Ant Hill Excavation had truly become a family affair. One of his daughters was currently operating heavy equipment. One of his sons was taking over the accounting, overseeing the part-time bookkeeper, and producing the financial reports and forecasts. The twins, both natural leaders, were working alongside Ant to assume what would eventually become co-CEO roles. Currently, both had titles of VP, as they had expressed early interest in the company and had the necessary educational backgrounds, as well as the practical experience from working with other organizations.

Ant knew his limitations as a CEO, and he knew that a major part of his role was to position the business for long-term growth. Someone had to be the chief strategist, the business development leader, and the manager of the overall operations of the company.

Ant knew he couldn't do everything or think of every possible scenario, and fortunately the twins were willing to step into those roles and assist him. Some of those scenarios kept him awake at night.

The specter of the pandemic hung over all of their heads. No one wanted to revisit the horror of the economic wasteland that existed after the shelter-in-place orders were lifted. Ant knew he and Grasshopper had to be prepared to pivot in response to any external threat or event.

Grasshopper had developed a "virtual events" revenue stream. Several of his kids were involved in facilitating company-wide meetings online, as well as workshops and social virtual gatherings. They had the technology ready and it provided a small revenue stream for the overall company. This pivot represented a response to the pandemic, and was value added overall as it was not depend on Grasshopper to generate revenue. Both Grasshopper and Ant were very alert to the dangers of creating revenue streams that were solely dependent on the CEO to thrive. The next steps for both Ant and Grasshopper were to determine what steps in these pivots could be translated to some other scenario. Ms. Ladybug had cautioned both Ant and Grasshopper about becoming "Business Is My Baby Owners" or BIMBO. Ant could see the dangers in thinking that because they had pandemics figured out, they didn't need to invest any time in exploring other scenarios that would help them create business continuity plans in the midst of those crises.

He was grateful to Ms. Ladybug for her advice, and he feared that Grasshopper had not absorbed all of her wisdom. Ant also knew that Grasshopper had not yet contacted a business coach. At their last meeting, Grasshopper had boasted of his ability to solve any problem. He had regaled Ant and Ms. Ladybug with stories of "near disasters" at certain events that Grasshopper managed to solve in ways that not only addressed the problems but also did so in a spectacularly dramatic manner that the clients ultimately loved. Ms. Ladybug had asked Grasshopper if his staff had had any input into the solutions, and she wondered what his team might have come up with if Grasshopper had not stepped in.

Grasshopper had laughed and replied that their solutions had not been nearly as imaginative as his, and that it had been a good thing that he had been there to "save the day." And, wasn't it wonderful that he turned these problems into opportunities? His quick thinking had prompted several of his clients to refer Grasshopper to business acquaintances planning large events. How excited Grasshopper had seemed! Ant wondered what Ms. Bee would say to that. He thought she might point out that Grasshopper had control issues, as a result of barely surviving the pandemic.

Ant could tell by Ms. Ladybug's expression that she was troubled by this perspective. He wondered if Grasshopper noticed, or even thought about, Ms. Ladybug's warnings about potential pitfalls. Ant talked about the work he had done with his coach, and he gave Grasshopper the coach's contact information a couple of times. Grasshopper had expressed his interest and need to hire someone to help as his business was growing by leaps and bounds. (Hmmm, that must be a Grasshopper kind of expression!)

Ant glanced at his watch. He realized that he'd spent the prior ten minutes in deep reflection, and there was still no sign of Grasshopper. Ant pulled out his Business Model Canvas plan, and his goals and objectives for the year, and focused for the next forty-five minutes on evaluating the relevance of those objectives within the scope of his three-year plan. Ant realized that several were important, but they didn't align as stated with the company's purpose or the three-year plan. Those that seemingly didn't fit, however, did align with the five-year plan. Ant highlighted those objectives for discussion with the board of directors.

Another check of the time. Okay, fifteen minutes before Ms. Ladybug would arrive. He then took out his calendar.

Ant and Grasshopper had on several occasions discussed the concept of "busy-ness" versus productive, revenue-generating activities. The two had decided to devote time each week to determine what percentage of their time was spent being "busy" and compare that to the time spent in productive, business-building activities. As he went back over his tally marks from each day, Ant realized that his ratio had improved. He was about fifty-fifty!

Ant went back to his notes from the meeting with Ms. Ladybug and Grasshopper the day they discussed this topic. He had forgotten (again) about breaking down his big tasks into shorter "bursts" of activity. There were strategic tasks he avoided simply because he had tagged those items as needing over sixty minutes each. Could he break those tasks down even further by making up a sequence of fifteen-minute steps to complete those tasks? He thought he could, which made each doable. In just a few minutes, Ant had broken down two of the items on his strategic planning objectives list and made a list of "easier to manage" fifteen-minute steps.

Just then, the door to the coffee shop opened, and in walked Ms. Ladybug. Ant jumped up, waved, and walked to greet her. He offered to buy her coffee when he bought himself a refill. As Ant came back to the table, Ms. Ladybug looked up and smiled at him. She gestured to the table, noting the evidence of his work. She then asked, "Where is Grasshopper?"

Ant responded with a shake of his head. "I don't know. I haven't seen him today. When we left off last week, he was in the midst of a crisis of some sort. He hasn't responded when I've reached out this week. I'm concerned about him, Ms. Ladybug. It occurred to me earlier this morning that he may have fallen into the BIMBO trap. I believe the trauma, associated with almost starving during the pandemic a few years ago, created a drive in Grasshopper to be in control at all times. What do you think?"

Ms. Ladybug nodded slowly. "You may be right. Do you remember when I met with the two of you last month, Grasshopper told us the story of his spectacular save during the big Locust Seventeen-Year Blowout? I almost challenged him then, and I probably should have in hindsight. It's true that he saved the situation, but he never asked for input from his team. He chose instead to use a command-and-control managerial mentality. As CEO, Grasshopper did not use the situation as a teaching and learning moment for his team. I believe it would've taken twenty minutes to call a quick onsite meeting to brainstorm options, have the team evaluate each with Grasshopper's oversight, and implement the best solution. Ant, have you noticed times when you behaved more as a manager and less as a CEO?"

Ant leaned back and nodded. He dropped his gaze and shifted in his seat. "Yes, I have. It's amazing to me how quickly I drop into parent mode with my grown children. Not only as a parent, mind you, but as a micromanaging, domineering taskmaster. It isn't pretty. Fortunately, I'm now open to the feedback that my children and colleagues are willing to offer. Sometimes the situation is one for the lesson journal. I screwed up, and it's over. At other times, we're able to collaboratively generate additional options that lead to a more efficient, and productive, outcome."

"How does that feel?" Ms. Ladybug went on to say, "I ask because since I've worked with a business coach, and have set up a board of directors, I have people both inside and outside of my organization to act as sounding boards for me, too. I cannot begin to describe how much that has changed my life as a person and as CEO."

Ant quickly asked, "What do you mean? How could those couple of changes make such a big difference?"

Ms. Ladybug smiled and nodded with understanding. "Okay, well, let me ask you about worry and anxiety. How much do you find yourself worrying or feeling anxious? Because I can tell you that for more than five long years worry and anxiety were like ever-present clouds over my head."

Ant shook his head, "Yeah, sure. Worry and stress are part of every day for me. I mean, I am a business owner with a growing business. Isn't that just part of the game?"

It was Ms. Ladybug's turn to shake her head. "No, that's actually a myth. Each of us can choose to operate that way, or not. You know, I gained a lot of insight from the book, *Traction*, by Gino Wickman on this topic. He devised the Entrepreneurial Operating System or *EOS*. Anyway, once I adopted a growth mindset, along with an expanded sense of awareness, I felt more open to the lessons that my advisors were willing to share. Their feedback helped — a lot! My decisions didn't feel so risky. I didn't spend my energy worrying about whether or not I had chosen the right one. I trusted my advisors, who felt comfortable advising me. It was a big win-win for me. I grew, and so did the business.

"Would you be surprised to learn that my stress level dropped, too? As the risk associated with decisions felt more manageable, I worried less. As I worried less, my energy went into evaluating and creating viable options. Some of those options generated unbelievable benefits. This approach became a sustainable system for me and my team. We became comfortable brainstorming. We used 'design thinking' in a playful way. The risks were minimal because we trusted each other to listen and riffed off of each other's ideas. This was another important evolution of my abilities to become a successful CEO and not just another manager who had created a job for herself and just a few others."

The two continued to discuss this idea. Ant listened with the intention to learn. They took a look at his list of activities. (Yes, the one Ant had used to determine the ratio of "busy manager" tasks to CEO tasks.) Ms. Ladybug offered a few suggestions on shifting those "busy manager" tasks over to others in the organization. The time flew.

As the two finished their discussion, they looked at the door. Still, there was no sign of Grasshopper. Ant sighed. "I think I should stop by Grasshopper's office after we leave here. The BIMBO habit sounds like a hard one to stop. The longer it goes on, the harder it sounds like it will be for Grasshopper to shift to new practices, if that is what he's doing. I'd also like to get next week's meeting on my calendar. Any chance you could join me?" Ms. Ladybug agreed.

Grasshopper was on the phone when Ant and Ms. Ladybug appeared. He was deep in conversation, so when he looked up, he was startled. Grasshopper had not realized that anyone had opened the door. He smiled at both and waved them to chairs in front of his desk. Grasshopper ended the call. He sat back, smiled, and blew out a long breath.

"Another disaster averted! Sorry I missed our meeting. As you heard, there was a problem, and I was caught in the middle. I couldn't leave and didn't think to notify you that I wouldn't make it." Grasshopper shrugged apologetically. He grinned sheepishly and proclaimed, "Look at us, living the life of an entrepreneur. Crazy, isn't it?"

Ms. Ladybug shook her head. "I don't agree, Grasshopper. I mean, it can be the life of an entrepreneur, if you want it to be. This is exactly what drove me to make the changes I made a few years ago. I am convinced that those changes are what led to the success — both financial and personal — that I enjoy today. I want to ask you, how well is this working for you? How well is this working for your team? What is Cricket's take on this?"

Grasshopper let out a dismissive snort. "Well, it's technically working, if you know what I mean. But, I'm not at all sure it's sustainable. And, well, Cricket quit yesterday. She told me that I treated her like a lackey, not as a valued member of the team. She accused me of undermining her authority during events. I mean, can I help it if I have the best ideas and am able to think on my feet during events? It's my gift!"

Ant leaned in and looked directly into Grasshopper's eyes. "Hey, don't you remember Ms. Ladybug talking about BIMBOs? You know, those owners who treat their businesses like their babies? Owners who create a business that only they can own and operate?" Ms. Ladybug nodded encouragingly at Ant. Ant continued, "Remember she shared with us the pitfall of using a managerial mentality instead of a CEO mindset. She cautioned us that the start of the business meant we had to wear every hat. But it's been over a year, and both of our businesses have passed out of the startup phase."

Ms. Ladybug spoke up, "Grasshopper, last month you told us

several stories about near disasters. You played a major role in each one, didn't you?" As Grasshopper nodded, Ms. Ladybug went on to ask, "What did your team learn from each of those situations? What kind of debrief, or after-action reporting, did you do with the team afterward?"

Grasshopper paused, then admitted that they hadn't done either. There were usually several events each weekend, and the team rolled from one event to the next. Everyone had a couple of days off after the events, returned to work, and started the whole rotation all over again. Grasshopper looked at both Ant and Ms. Ladybug. "Do you do something like this, Ant, after your projects are completed?" Ant nodded. Then, Grasshopper asked, "How does this help? I mean the job is done. What does this investment of time and energy get you, especially after the fact?"

Ms. Ladybug answered his question, "Currently, it looks as though you've given yourself a job as a manager who solves problems. You step in as soon as you recognize an issue. I'd like to challenge you to consider what you are teaching and modeling for your team. How will you use this business model to grow? Is this business model sustainable, and can it scale? Finally, how will you shift from a managerial mentality to a CEO mindset?"

Ant then spoke up. "Grasshopper, it looks like you are the hub of the team. You've set yourself up as the problem solver. You're teaching your team to step back when there's a problem so that you can handle it. Isn't that going to impede your company's ability to grow? Who will act as the CEO of your company if you are also acting as everyone's manager? You've said you want to sell this business at some point. I don't see how this company becomes an asset of interest to good buyers if you're the manager and problem solver who has to be on-site at every event to oversee it because your team isn't equipped to make decisions or address issues that always seem to come up. Ms. Ladybug warned us about this months ago. You've got to turn this around. What are you willing to do about this?"

Grasshopper looked up at the ceiling and closed his eyes. He took a deep breath, let it out, and dropped his shoulders. He picked his head up and asked, "How much time do the two of you have? I need help in thinking this through. I don't think I can do this by myself."

Over the next hour, Ms. Ladybug, Ant, and Grasshopper reviewed Grasshopper's business plan, values, purpose, mission, goals, and objectives. The three came up with a script for framing a conversation with his team before an event and scheduling a debrief for the day the team was back in the office following the event. Also, Grasshopper called the business coach, Ms. Bee, and made an appointment. As the three concluded that they had gotten as far as they could that day, Ms. Ladybug asked Grasshopper, "How do you feel?"

Grasshopper paused and then replied, "Like a fool. Ant, you were right. Ms. Ladybug did caution us about becoming BIMBOs. I remember it but didn't think it applied to me. I also recognize that I get a lot out of jumping in and solving a problem at an event. It feeds my ego, you know? It makes me feel like a hero in front of the client and the team. Of course, that is the immediate gain that actually costs Wingsong in the long run. Thank you both for taking the time to work with me through this stuff. I really needed the shift in perspective."

"One more thing, Grasshopper. Ms. Ladybug and I discussed the need to be diligent about keeping score on the number of times we act with a managerial mentality versus the number of times we approach a situation using a CEO mindset. I will come up with a scorecard for us to use and send it to you. Also, let's schedule our next accountability appointment, okay?"

And the Moral of the Story is... *Don't be a BIMBO!*

So, we have an important new concept for you, faithful fable reader — "BIMBO," which stands for "Business Is My Baby Owner"

syndrome. This happens when owners feel like they are the only ones who can be trusted to manage the business. When there is a problem with a customer, this type of owner steps in to solve it. If there is a supply chain disruption, or an operations system failure, this owner is right there, ready to offer a solution.

The business becomes a mirror image of the owner. It reflects the owner's skills, strengths, weaknesses, and blind spots. In these situations, the business is generally NOT valuable to a prospective buyer. We have seen this time and again in our client practices. Owners believe that because the income statement shows a profit, the business is of value to prospective buyers. Unfortunately, prospective buyers not only want to buy a profitable company, but they also want the company to thrive under new ownership.

To achieve this, build your company so that you are eventually out of a job. Scale, and empower a skilled management team. Build systems and processes that function distinctly from specific people. Create role descriptions that include attributes, desirable strengths, skills, and opportunities for future growth. Value your people as part of your legacy and culture. We encourage you to monitor the synergies across all aspects of your business so that as a whole, it becomes a valuable asset either for a buyer or the next generation.

In Gino Wickman's book, *Traction*, he describes *EOS* (the Entrepreneurial Operating System). We recommend this book to clients who are interested in building their companies to either sell, to seek financing, or to pass onto future generations.

Earlier in this chapter, Ant and Grasshopper are challenged to shift their perspectives to that of a CEO. We've included a scorecard at the end of this chapter that we encourage you to download and use to calculate your ratio of managerial mentality to CEO mindset activities. It's a great exercise to do for a couple of weeks, several times a year. Also, those of you who are in startup mode may want to calculate the ratio of tasks that serve to keep you busy versus those that generate revenue (and some of those tasks, of course, will be in both categories). Both of these exercises can offer insights into your EOS.

Another useful resource is the book, *The 12 Week Year*, by Brian Moran. Moran makes the case for viewing each quarter as a "year" for goal setting. Ant may have found this valuable as he looked at the alignment of his plan's goals and objectives. Clients have found this useful for keeping track of their own goals, objectives, and outcomes.

While the following may seem obvious, a surprising number of business owners make decisions in isolation and neglect viewing their companies through the lens of a prospective buyer. Here is an example from another area of life that many of us can relate to. Wendy recently learned about a family who owned a really beautiful old farmhouse in upstate New York. From what she was told, the house had been added onto over a number of years, somewhat haphazardly.

Apparently, a past owner had wanted to add a bathroom to the second floor. That owner had constructed a second-floor bathroom, but totally missed the ultimate purpose for it. Unfortunately, you couldn't access the bathroom from the second floor. Second-floor guests had to go downstairs, and then up the back staircase to get to that bathroom. Once done, back down and around to the main staircase to get back to the second-floor guest room. That's crazy, isn't it? How did that past owner justify the expense and effort of an additional, wonky bathroom that the guests couldn't access while on the second floor? Yes, there was another bathroom, which buyers generally like. But, did it really meet the needs of a future owner?

As an owner, your job is to make sure that YOU aren't building wonky bathrooms. Build systems and processes that make sense to the entire team and to your outside advisors. Utilize your board, business coach, accountability partner, and mentors to test your ideas. Engage in scenario planning with the whole team using those systems and processes. Will they stand the test of a pandemic, climate event, or the absence of the owner? This process will allow those in positions of responsibility to know the possible changes to the business model, operations, and the recovery plan.

If you are busy wearing every hat, your limited perspectives may not reflect the experiences that you are trying to deliver to your customers, employees, or potential buyers. Wendy recommends a form of design thinking to generate options. Here is one version of the steps from the Interactive Design Foundation:

1. Empathize - Research Your Users' Needs.
2. Define - State Your Users' Needs and Problems.
3. Ideate - Challenge Assumptions and Create Ideas.
4. Prototype - Start to Create Solutions.
5. Test - Try Your Solutions Out.

We recognize that this requires a willingness to be transparent and vulnerable. There has to be a degree of trust for that transparency to be beneficial and profitable. Ant and Grasshopper started with a common purpose — to grow businesses. The trust and transparency between them, and their relationship, continue to develop over time.

In the beginning, it appeared that both were convinced that their way of operating a business was the "right" way to do things. We see that Ant confessed to believing that Grasshopper would have little to teach him. Ant thought this would be a one-sided arrangement with Grasshopper receiving all of the benefits. In hindsight, Ant recognized that this was an ego-based belief. We already know that Ant owned up to feeling fear and vowed not to live a fear-based life. We haven't heard him acknowledge shame or vulnerability, but we suspect they are both there.

Emotions can make a major impact on decisions. As a business owner, it's your responsibility to process your emotions so that you can access your instincts. Shame and vulnerability carry a lot of weight in many decisions. Both are hard to process. Unprocessed emotions impact your perspective, as well as the ability to make sound decisions. If Ant is correct in thinking that Grasshopper was traumatized by the pandemic's economic fallout (he almost starved, didn't he?), then Grasshopper could cope by assuming control in all dicey situations. It may feel better to him to be the problem solver, than to feel the vulnerability and risk associated with depending on another's ability to solve the problem.

One of Wendy's clients carried shame each time she asked for help. Empowering her team was challenging for this owner because it meant acknowledging that there were limitations to what she could reasonably accomplish by herself, despite the fact that her business was not profitable. For a time, this client lost sight of the freedom and strength found in creating an empowered team. Coaching helped the client release this long-held belief to grow as a CEO. This is just one example of the wisdom of having the right combination of outside advisors. The financial investment made to pay for outside advisors is worthwhile if the result is growth, development, greater profitability, and more fun in your life.

It sounds counterintuitive to encourage business owners to work themselves out of a position, doesn't it? However, this objective allows the company to grow as an entity that is sustainable and independent of the owner well into the future. Think about it — if your company functions well without you, a prospective buyer or strategic partner will likely be able to envision how your company might fit within their vision. If, however, the company is dependent on you as the "go-to man or woman" for everything, it isn't nearly as easy to get comfortable with buying your company.

Here's another value added perspective on empowering your team and nurturing your team's talent. You can take pride and a great deal of satisfaction in the successes of those you've mentored, and led. Your leadership guides the people on your team through decision making, problem solving and creative ideas to generate results that the entire company can be proud of. It takes putting aside your own ego to let others take the credit while you take responsibility.

If this sounds, or feels, threatening to you as a business owner, consider spending some time creating a vision for life outside and apart from your company. This is another situation in which a coach can be of great value. Take the time to invest in the next phase of your life to determine possible paths to pursue. Then, consider whether those paths align with your values, interests, and strengths. Explore the possible challenges and obstacles to each while you develop strategies to mitigate the risks and capitalize on the opportunities.

Below is a scorecard you can use to track your activities as either a Managerial Mentality or a CEO Mindset. At the end of a week or so, reflect on how you can shift those situations to land solidly in the CEO Mindset category.

CEO Mindset Scorecard

This is a tool for ongoing assessment. Check in with yourself regularly to assess your progress as a leader, not just a manager.

Are you using a managerial mentality or a CEO Mindset?

What assumptions have you carried into the situation?

What patterns or habits do you continue to engage in using?

How can you gain greater understanding of the situation?

What do you need to successfully convert this situation into an opportunity??

SITUATION

Describe:

Check each that applies:
Manager Mentality
CEO Mindset
Generous Assumptions
Seeking to understand

Where can you improve?

SITUATION

Describe:

Check each that applies:
Manager Mentality
CEO Mindset
Generous Assumptions
Seeking to understand

Where can you improve?

In addition, we've also shared a Disaster Preparation & Recovery Guide for business owners and their teams. Remember, if you need help contact your coach, mentor, or Board members. You can find the PDF of this at www.ascendcoachingsolutions.com.

THE BUSINESS OF DISASTER PREPARATION & RECOVERY

1 **PREPARE TO RESPOND, NOT REACT**
Owners, CEO's, the Team, Board Members, & Advisors compare & share the business landscape as each sees it.

2 **EQUIPPED FOR ANYTHING**
Develop a bias for action. Create systems & processes for decision-making & assessments. Cut costs. Generate revenue.

3 **ACCEPT REALITY: USE YOUR POWER**
Climate changes, pandemics, war, economic crashes - each is a disruption in the market, industry & culture. Own it.

4 **SURVIVE TO THRIVE**
Companies can be leaders in the midst of disaster pivoting to meet the future. Create opportunity from disaster.

ASCEND COACHING SOLUTIONS

BETTER LIFE, BETTER BUSINESS COACHING
WWW.ASCENDCOACHINGSOLUTIONS.COM

THE BUSINESS OF DISASTER PREPARATION & RECOVERY

5 **TACTICS FOR SURVIVAL**
Devise potential pivots to the business model that align with the company's vision, values, mission/purpose, & goals.

6 **LEAD THE DISCUSSIONS**
Explore changes to the operating plan. Look for weaknesses & strengths within the organization. Leverage the strengths.

7 **LOOK FOR OPPORTUNITIES**
Integrate current market, industry & economic data. Identify streams of revenue, cut costs, and watch cash flow.

8 **SURVIVAL PIVOTS**
Review changes to the business model, plans of operation and utilize scenario plans. Implement & execute.

ASCEND COACHING SOLUTIONS

BETTER LIFE, BETTER BUSINESS COACHING
WWW.ASCENDCOACHINGSOLUTIONS.COM

4

KEEP YOUR EYES ON THE PRIZE

*Fun Facts: Ants have compound eyes, and grasshoppers have five eyes!
And a group of ladybugs is called a loveliness.*

So much had happened in the three and a half years since Ant and Grasshopper met for the first time at the coffee shop when each decided to start a business! Both had left the startup phase of business and transitioned to the growth and development stages. Both Ant Hill Excavations and Wingsong Events had family members working in the companies. Today, at their annual strategic planning meeting, Ant and Grasshopper were connecting with Ms. Ladybug, their mentor, who was hosting them at her offices.

As Ant made his way to the meeting, he reflected on the past few years. He smiled to himself as he opened the door and stepped inside Ms. Ladybug's office building. She, too, had grown her company, and he planned to ask her to explain more about her growth strategies. Ms. Ladybug came into the reception area as he closed the outer door.

"Hi, Ant! How are you today?" greeted Ms. Ladybug. "I am well, thank you, Ms. Ladybug," replied Ant. "Have you seen my accountability partner yet?"

"No, I haven't. But, as usual, you are early, and Grasshopper... well, let's just say that late is his SOP." While we wait, want to come in and get settled?" Ms. Ladybug bustled around the conference room, adjusting the temperature and checking the whiteboard. "I'm going to get water and coffee for us. I'll be right back, Ant," said Ms. Ladybug.

Ant looked around the room as he placed his bag in a chair and Ms. Ladybug walked out to get the coffee and water. At the end of the first year, the three had decided to spend at least one day each year planning for the year ahead, reviewing the past year, and running scenario plans. They agreed it was an extremely valuable exercise.

The three of them had hatched plans and launched initiatives from this very table for the last couple of years. Ant looked forward to whatever this day would bring for his company. Just then, he heard sounds out in the reception area. He looked out into the hallway and spotted Grasshopper. He seemed to be in a hurry. No surprise there!

Ant called out, "Hey, Grasshopper! How are you? Everything okay? I was so worried when you were late." Grasshopper looked up in surprise and then detected the smirk on Ant's face. "No, you weren't! You know I make the most of every minute, so I'm a little late."

Grasshopper tossed his bag into a chair and plopped down. He sighed as he said, "What a day, and it's only 8:00 am! I hope this session is as good as the last couple have been for my business. I need a plan, and Wingsong needs a *profitable* plan at that! Where's Ms. Ladybug? Is she here yet?"

"Of course, she's here!" Ant replied. "She's getting coffee and water for us. Hey, did you get a chance to look around when you walked in? Ms. Ladybug seems to have carried out each of her initiatives from the last meeting. I think I saw a new *Loveliness Construction* truck parked out front! She has her company logo on it, with a banner that highlights her maintenance and repair services. I also saw a new ad in the newspaper just last week."

Grasshopper nodded approvingly. "I noticed those things, too. Ms. Ladybug certainly seems to have carried out each of her intentions from the last planning meeting!"

"Yeah, and did you see that new building out back? I'll bet that's her new training and development classroom. I think I saw a flyer on the bulletin board for machine and tool safety classes as I walked back here. I wonder if she's on track to offer the other classes that she wants to provide!? Training and development for her guys is high on the list as she hires to retain skilled employees. I wonder if she's managed to get the virtual classes up?"

Grasshopper leaned forward and put his elbows on the table. "She's brilliant! These ideas are innovative."

Ant agreed, saying, "And it's a great investment in her people."

Just then Ms. Ladybug came bustling in with the water and the carafe of coffee. "Hey, Grasshopper! How are you? I'm so glad to see you! Did you happen to see my new service truck in the yard, and the learning and development classroom? You both may remember that training and development for my team is high on my list — and I'm working to increase the online offerings of the trainings. And I am on my way to two new revenue streams, too!"

Both Ant and Grasshopper praised Ms. Ladybug on her progress. They raised their mugs in salute as the three celebrated her success. Then, Ms. Ladybug suggested that they begin their strategy session.

Standing in front of the whiteboard, Ms. Ladybug said, "Let's review our top five values and our vision statements. What changes do we want to make to those?"

"My values list has not changed since last year. Ant, as I recall, you and I put family and prosperity in our top five values the past few years. That stays the same for me, as well as the fun, leisure, and love. How about the two of you?" asked Grasshopper. The three discussed the differences and similarities among their values lists. This was their annual review of not only their personal values but also the values they intend to use for their companies.

Ms. Ladybug leaned forward, "I used this list recently in a new way. You know I've identified the shortage of skilled labor as one of the challenges my company will face for at least the next five years. It's frustrating to hire someone, invest in their training, and have them leave before there is any real return on the investment, right?" She looked up, and both Ant and Grasshopper nodded knowingly.

"Well, last week I started to get together whatever I might need for our meeting today, and I happened to pull out my values lists. During the interview I had scheduled for that afternoon, I asked the candidate to describe different situations to illustrate her people skills. At the end of each, I asked the candidate to describe why that was a good representation of her skills. The amazing part was that I was able to identify the candidate's values. I then confirmed my assessment by discussing the topic with the candidate."

She took a sip of coffee and continued. "I felt really good about that interview and offered her the job. Only time will tell if she is the right person for the job, of course. But I do know that including values in my hiring process allowed me to determine whether or not this person held the same values as the company. It also helped me to explore whether there were any conflicting values." Ms. Ladybug sat back and smiled at Ant and Grasshopper.

Ant looked thoughtful and then spoke up. "You know, that is really interesting," said Ant. "I actually had an unexpected development last week, and ended up using my values list, too, but in an entirely different way. I had a call from someone out of state who was interested in buying my company. As you all know, at the last strategy meeting, I decided to include selling as a possible option for exiting. But not this soon, of course! Anyway, I was completely taken by surprise. I stuttered through 'I'll take a pass, but thanks,' and ended the call. I have no idea how much Ant Hill Excavation is worth today. At this point my company's valuation is a couple of years old. That taught me an important lesson — be prepared!"

Ant looked at both as he continued, "While I don't intend to sell right now, I do want to build the company and exit at some point. I believe that my kids will want to buy me out and take over. But, who knows what will happen in the future? So, I pulled out my values list and came up with a script for future calls that uses my core values in the conversation.

"The call made me realize something else, too. I'm still using the same attorney and accountants that you referred me to when I first started out, Ms. Ladybug. I don't think either one has experience in buying or selling businesses, however. The whole thing started me thinking. So, I also reached out to a couple of M&A bankers and used the opportunity to see if my values and theirs align. If I should decide to sell, I feel good about how to have those initial conversations — all because I know what my priorities are, and why."

Grasshopper blinked; his eyes wide. "Jumping Juniper, Ant! Wow, I don't know how much my business is worth either. I intend to find out, though. I had a meeting with the commercial loan officer at my bank. He was very helpful and explained how best to go about getting an independent valuation. You know, I use the same attorney and accountant that you use. So, I'd love to be in on those future meetings for my networking purposes." Grasshopper turned his gaze to Ms. Ladybug.

"Ms. Ladybug, your story makes me wonder how I could better use my values to hire and to promote. Things have been stable with my events business for the past year, but I'm still too involved in the day-to-day operations." Grasshopper looked sheepish as he glanced from Ms. Ladybug to Ant.

"The irony is I vowed to both of you last year that by this time I would have stepped out of a number of those roles. But, um, I haven't. I'm in danger of building something that only I can lead, and that has to change. That is one of my goals for today — to take a hard look at how to implement and execute that strategy."

Grasshopper's face lit up as he spoke, "On the other hand, in working with my accountant and financial planner, I'd also like to set another goal for myself this year. I'd like to expand my business and buy another. In fact, I already have several strategic partners that appear to be good acquisition candidates. With that said, the guy at the bank told me that while strategic acquisitions can increase value, the vast majority don't unless the numbers, the people, and the cultures are a fit." Ms. Ladybug and Ant exchanged skeptical looks, which Grasshopper noticed.

Grasshopper put both of his hands in the air and said, "I know, I know! How can I talk about acquiring another company, when I haven't worked out my role in my own company? The bank wasn't happy about that, either. That's why I need to make the changes this year in my role." He paused. "You know, it's only in the past six months that I've come to truly appreciate the dangers of being a BIMBO."

Grasshopper shook his head and sighed. "Thanks to working with Ms. Bee, I've realized that I'm a BIMBO in part because I fear not being in control. At first, I denied it. Then, I realized I really hate to hand over control to anybody else. I also want to thank the two of you for being on this journey with me. I shudder to think where I'd be today without your support." Ant smiled.

Ms. Ladybug leaned forward excitedly. "Guess what? I have a surprise for the two of you. I have invited Mr. Walking Stick, an investment banker, and Ms. Butterfly, a part-time or fractional CFO, to come and talk with us this afternoon. Both have experience with mergers and acquisitions. I believe it would be a great idea for the three of us to understand what our options are for our exits, as well as how to shift our perspectives from looking at our businesses as owners to prospective buyers. What do you think?"

Ant and Grasshopper looked at one another and then back at Ms. Ladybug. "Wow! That is a generous idea! Ms. Ladybug, thank you so much for putting this together."

Grasshopper looked excited. "When do they arrive? I'm ready!" He was ready to hop into it!

Ms. Ladybug shook her head. "Grasshopper, we have several hours of work to do before they get here. We need to spend some time looking at the past year, then do a debrief." Ms. Ladybug walked to the whiteboard.

"Let's follow our usual annual strategy meeting formula:

- What are our goals for the next year?
- What are the numbers?
- How do the actual numbers stack up against our forecasts?
- What are our goals for next year? In three years? In five years?

After we've covered all of those topics, let's add in these activities:

- Develop timelines for our business 'cycles.' We will put each major yearly task and event on a timeline.
- Add the major ups and downs for our businesses that seem to happen every year.

- Let's also add in the major life events we see on the horizon for the next decade.
- Then, let's identify a couple of timeframes that may make sense for us to exit.
- From there, let's highlight the time it would take to prepare our teams for an ownership transition. Let's include things like the 'grief' period, systems/processes integration, and our transitions as leaders.

Grasshopper's eyes widened dramatically. "How in the hell can we do all of that? We don't have any idea when things are going to happen in our lives. That sounds like a lot of planning for nothing." Ms. Ladybug shook her head. "Grasshopper, when would you ideally like to retire?"

"Um, in the next five to ten years — I hope," he answered.

"Okay, then, you will note that on the timeline." Ms. Ladybug continued writing on the whiteboard and asked:

- How about your wife? When will she retire from the company?
- When do your kids finish school?
- Is anybody engaged or planning to move out?
- What are your younger kids' plans for careers?
- What are the kids' expectations for the business? And have you communicated your plans?

"I could go on, and I will add more questions later. But, for now, my question to you is how much would it help you to look at all of these events and put them on a timeline?"

"I believe that looking at this stuff could help us a lot!" said Ant. Grasshopper said, "Let's get to it!"

The three leaned into their work and didn't break until it was time for lunch. Each looked forward to the arrival of Mr. Walking Stick and Ms. Butterfly.

Ant and Grasshopper had decided to order in. Ms. Ladybug

offered each a space to eat, check emails, and call in to their offices. The hour sped by while they caught up on the events of the day so far. Ant walked into the break room and started to gather up his trash. He paused in front of Grasshopper, who was on the phone, and pointed to his watch. It sounded like Grasshopper was deep into some crisis or another. He issued orders with detailed instructions to whoever was on the phone.

Ant shook his head. Grasshopper had a long way to go as far as stepping out of his role as chief problem solver for Wingsong Events. BIMBO all the way! He turned and headed back to the conference room. Ant heard Grasshopper begin to wrap up the conversation, but then he dove right back into command-and-control mode. Ant sighed.

When Ant rounded the corner and re-entered the conference room, he saw their guests. He extended his hand while he introduced himself to Mr. Walking Stick and Ms. Butterfly, who did the same. Ms. Ladybug entered next, noted that Grasshopper was absent, and turned to Ant with a lifted eyebrow. "Well?" she inquired.

Ant poked his head out of the room and listened down the hall. "I believe he's coming. Let me just give him another signal," offered Ant. He hurried down the hall towards Grasshopper's voice. He stopped, stood in front of Grasshopper, and crossed his arms over his chest while he glared at him. Grasshopper looked up, saw the look on Ant's face, and immediately said to the person he was talking to, "Look, I've gotta go. Just do what I'd do, and you'll be fine. I will see you at about 6:00 pm."

Grasshopper popped up and came around the desk. "I'm sorry. I'm on my way right now." Ant responded by using his paternal voice, "It is rude to keep our guests waiting."

Suddenly Ant stopped and turned around to face Grasshopper. "Sorry about the tone, Grasshopper. I just realized I spoke to you like I speak to my grown children at Anthill Excavation, and that isn't good. Hey, I'm really concerned! When are you planning to empower your team and step out of problem-solving? In ten years?

The bigger the company gets, the harder it will be. Twenty? Thirty? Never?!" Ant put an arm around his friend's shoulder, "Wake up! Today is the day! You need to break that habit!"

The two entered the room, and another round of introductions took place. Ant, Grasshopper, and Ms. Ladybug sat back with pen in hands to listen and learn as Mr. Walking Stick and Ms. Butterfly spent the next hour describing the process of buying and selling a business. With years of experience as an investment banker, Mr. Walking Stick went through the steps, the costly pitfalls, and what prospective buyers and investors look for in a valuable enter-prise. Grasshopper squirmed when Mr. Walking Stick cited owners who not only did not have a handle on their numbers but also built their businesses primarily around their own skills without devel-oping the management team. Mr. Walking Stick was very clear, "BIMBOs don't sell!" Ant caught Grasshopper's eye and raised his eyebrow.

Ms. Butterfly then described her role in working with clients as a fractional CFO. She emphasized how important it is for business owners to know their numbers. Ms. Butterfly assisted clients in knowing their numbers and company value. Ant had heard of this type of relationship, but he didn't know any of the details.

"My clients hire me to provide financial leadership and over-sight, but in a part-time capacity," she explained. "I can advise clients on capital expenditures, financing, and assist in assessing value." As they had been colleagues for many years, Mr. Walking Stick spoke up several times to emphasize the value that Ms. Butterfly brings to a potential transaction.

"With Ms. Butterfly's help, the client's books are clean, easy to follow, and act as supporting documentation in a transaction," he stated. Both Mr. Walking Stick and Ms. Butterfly outlined the chal-lenges of integrating companies that had done their own books, without using third-party advisors or best practices.

Taking turns with their inquiries, Ant, Grasshopper, and Ms. Ladybug each had questions and engaged Mr. Walking Stick and Ms. Butterfly, who stayed another hour to address each topic in some detail. At the end of the time with their guests, Mr. Walking Stick and Ms. Butterfly shared the whiteboard.

Ms. Butterfly began, "We want to leave you with these recommendations, and as business owners, always be sure to keep the following in mind." They wrote the following:

- Know your numbers!
- Complete an independent audit of your company at least every three to five years, depending on the level of change in your business and industry. Plan for an independent valuation prior to succession, selling your business, or buying another business.
- Learn as much as you can about the mergers and acquisitions ("M&A") process.
- Develop your exit strategy, and then communicate it to your stakeholders. For example, don't wait until you are ready to exit before communicating your plans to your family, key employees, and board!
- Empower your team.
- While in the midst of selling your business, you will be expected to hit your sales and operating income forecasts. If you don't, it will affect the purchase price!
- It is very important to deliver the due diligence information requested in a timely manner. Be sure to answer all calls and emails promptly and communicate clearly with advisors and the prospective buyer.
- Designate someone to act as the primary point of contact with the buyer during the sale process and be aware that this is the equivalent of a full-time job for at least several months.
- Lastly, you as the seller need to be very clear about your desired outcome for the sale process. For example, do you want to stay on as a consultant, assume another role in the organization, or leave the company altogether?

Ms. Butterfly and Mr. Walking Stick were genuinely glad to see that the trio was listening closely and taking copious notes. Mr. Walking Stick then said, "If you'd like, Ms. Butterfly and I would like to introduce the three of you to several attorneys, business brokers, and accountants with M&A experience."

All three smiled, and Ms. Ladybug said, "That's very generous of you. Thank you! We would really like that."

As everyone rose to say goodbye, Ms. Butterfly offered one last recommendation. "It can be tempting to rationalize using only online accounting software and a tax accountant for the life of your business. As you know, that approach can be both cost-effective and simple. However, be aware that some potential risks with this approach may not appear until much later when you want to sell! And sometimes they become apparent when it's too late to change course. So, consider adding a fractional CFO to your team once your business reaches the $2–3 million revenue level." Ms. Butterfly nodded to each, and she then left the room with Mr. Walking Stick.

Grasshopper looked at Ms. Ladybug and Ant, pursed his lips, and blew out a long breath. "Well, I don't know about you two, but I've got a lot of clean up to do. Let's move on to the actionable steps that we need to take to implement our strategies, and I really need your help!"

Impressed, Ant smiled, reached out to slap Grasshopper on the shoulder, and asked, "What can I do to help you succeed? And, what can you do to support me? I feel like I have as many items on my to-do list as the two of you."

Ms. Ladybug nodded and said, "Okay, wasn't that great meeting with them? Let's make a list of our goals and the steps we need to take to achieve each. From there, let's share the goals and steps to get some feedback from the group. Sound good?" Both Ant and Grasshopper nodded in agreement, and the three used the next two hours to complete their goal-setting tasks.

Grasshopper then asked Ant and Ms. Ladybug, "May I ask you a favor? I really need accountability support during our weekly meetings. It's way past time for me to extricate myself from the day-to-day operations of the business." Ant and Ms. Ladybug agreed to support him, and it was shaping up to be another quick year for the three of them!

And the Moral of the Story is....*You have to name it to claim it!*

Along with two close friends, Preston and Lori Campbell, we started a company called Document Warehouse in the late 1990s. Document Warehouse provided off-site records management services (storage, retrieval, and destruction) to the healthcare and other end markets. Lori is an amazing graphic designer who handled the branding. JD had the investment banking experience, and Wendy provided the therapeutic touch, reminding us all about our commitment to our friendship and the goal of selling to a larger strategic buyer, like Iron Mountain. (As a former therapist now coach, Wendy brings a therapeutic touch to her business coaching clients.) Preston devoted the most time and energy to the business as the president and day-to-day leader. He was driven and determined, which benefitted us all.

We ultimately had the good fortune to sell to the best prospective buyer, which was Iron Mountain. At the time, Iron Mountain was the most active consolidator in the records management industry. While we didn't get rich, we learned a lot, we made a profit, and we are still close friends today. We used our intention to sell and the desire to maintain our friendship as our guardrails for making decisions. Preston knew that Iron Mountain was our best potential acquirer. So, systems and processes were designed to fit with Iron Mountain. Overall, it was a big success for the four of us.

Not long ago, Wendy had the opportunity to work with a client who came to one of her sessions and was facing a challenge with a team member. As they worked through the issue, the owner realized that what had started as a "direct report" relationship had become more of a friendship. The friendship helped the working relationship in some respects but also complicated it by blurring the boundaries between their respective roles.

The client and Wendy began by revisiting the work that was accomplished in a previous session. They looked at the prioritized values, the goals for the company, and those for this direct report. The client had also developed an outline of the attributes of an ideal leader and had worked to embody that ideal. The client and Wendy then role-played a conversation about the key relationship issues, using the client's values, goals, and leadership ideals as guardrails. The client rated the session as a 'io out of io' and went on to successfully reset the relationship to retain the best aspects of both the working relationship and the friendship.

While this was not, and will not be, a 'one and done' kind of conversation, it's definitely worth the investment of the client's time. My client has identified this team member as a high-potential individual in the organization. Replacing this person would be costly both to the company and to the client. While it can be messy to dig into these issues, the benefits can be huge. What are the costs, you might ask? Consider these:

- Personnel losses and the associated grief at the company and the impact on the culture can greatly impact productivity and be a major distraction.
- When a key employee leaves, others in the organization have to pick up the extra work, along with reviewing resumes, interviewing, and ultimately onboarding the replacement.
- As a specific example, an employee making $10 per hour will cost more than $3,000 to replace. [1]

It is so gratifying to write about business owners who actually sit down once a year to strategize and plan their exits. We discuss best practices with our clients regularly. However, typically when we walk into a networking event, we note that the vast majority of business owners have only the vaguest notion of what selling their businesses would entail. This is so surprising considering that the large majority of business owners plan to use the proceeds from the sale of their businesses to fund their retirement!

So, when exactly do they (and you) plan to get started? Most say, "When the time is right." Wow! In our experience, there is no "perfect" time for busy people to do this critical work. If you don't do the work ahead of time, the M&A market may be hot, but you may not be ready to pursue a transaction. Even worse, what if you or your spouse develops a health issue, and you need to sell, but you aren't prepared? In short, it is easy to be lured into the trap of thinking that you have "years and years" before you need to develop an exit plan, but the future often comes at us far faster than we expect.

In 2020 the world was faced with the COVID-19 pandemic. The year started with a very robust stock market with key foundational elements of the economy rated as strong. Once the virus spread to the US, the market declined, businesses shut down, and millions of people lost their jobs and filed for unemployment.

One of my clients had a brick-and-mortar business. In just six weeks, she moved her entire inventory online, created virtual lessons, shopping experiences, and community meetups on her FB page. This business owner filed for the PPP Loan and then recalled furloughed employees who had chosen to work as volunteers to get the online store up and running. Not only has this business owner survived the pandemic, but she also has a recovery plan that she's put into action. This owner used a terrible situation to build value within her business.

I believe profit, people, and scenario planning are essential for longevity in business. Be ready. Build resilience.

I'd like to share one last scenario with you, which is also one from real life. We spoke with Michele Wink of UP Professional Solutions last August on the fourteenth anniversary of Hurricane Katrina. UP was a division of the engineering firm that Michele's father started in the 1970s in New Orleans. The parent company ultimately became the largest engineering firm in Louisiana.

This family business had five members of the second generation working at the company, as well as a succession plan, but they did not have a climate preparedness plan. While this may not have been a high priority in the early days of the business, with the benefit of hindsight, we can all easily understand the huge risk that it ultimately presented for the company.

As a result, several years after Hurricane Katrina hit New Orleans, the company had to be sold "under pressure" for a below market valuation because client contracts dried up before the government recovery funds kicked in. Michele and her family were very generous in sharing their wisdom and experiences from this painful story with us. They did a lot of things according to best practices, but this is one key element that they missed.

As we close this chapter, we would like to offer you the Values Assessment that we use with our clients. Use the Values Assessment shared below to chart the alignment between your personal values and the values exhibited by your company. You can either complete this in your journal using two different colored pens or visit our website at www.ascendcoachingsolutions.com for the form template. Circle all of the values that resonate with you. Circle values that actually <u>exist</u> in your life, not the ones you <u>wish</u> you had. Then, choose the four most important values, and prioritize them, starting with the most important at the top of the list. Then, use another colored pen to repeat the exercise for your <u>company</u>.

Consider how each of the prioritized values show up in your life and in your business. If you have a decision to make that is proving to be difficult, ask yourself how the options do or do not align with your values. Going forward, we recommend that you make it a standard practice to use your values as one of the guardrails in decision making as you build your company.

VALUES ASSESSMENT

Circle the values that resonate with you. Choose 4 of the values you circled. Prioritize by placing the most important at the top, least important at the bottom of the list.

VALUE #1:

VALUE #2:

VALUE #3:

VALUE #4:

accomplishment	abundance	achievement	faith	generosity
adventure	altruism	autonomy	acceptance	genius
beauty	clarity	commitment	awareness	honor
communication	community	connecting to others	capability	hard work
love	health	environment	candor	humility
family	flexibility	excellence	compassion	independence
friendship	fulfillment	freedom	empathy	innovation
holistic living	humor	fun	consciousness	insightful
honesty	integrity	intimacy	courage	intuitive
joy	leadership	loyalty	dependability	justice
nature	openness	orderliness	drive energy	kindness
personal growth	partnership	physical appearance	enthusiasm	organization
power	privacy respect	professionalism	fidelity	patience
recognition	self-care	romance	fairness	selfless
security	self-realization	sensuality	status	spontaneous
self-mastery	spirituality	trust	grace	strength
service	vitality	comfort		tough
truth	love			

TUNE YOUR ANTENNAE TO SUCCESS

Fun Fact: Antennae are used for smell, detection, feeling hot or cold and listening. They work on, in and through the environment.

I t was a beautiful morning. As Grasshopper glanced at his watch, he realized that he was running late — again. He hurried to gather up the documents he wanted to use for the yearly strategic meeting at Jitterbug Brewery with Ant and Ms. Ladybug. Ant found it hard to believe that another year had passed, and it was time to have another strategic planning meeting. Time is truly flying by! Ant realized that each year the planning that he, Grasshopper, and Ms. Ladybug played an important role in the growth of each company. They would have the place to themselves while they worked on their businesses.

Jitterbug was one of Wingsong's favorite venues for events. Grasshopper planned to work on his strategic plan with Ant and Ms. Ladybug, while the brewery staff prepared for his company's next big client social to be held there later that week. He felt very smart to have lined up the timing so that he could accomplish two things simultaneously.

He enjoyed that feeling for a moment more. Then, his mind went to the last time he worked an event at Jitterbug and the very uncomfortable clash with two of his employees. Those two employees also happened to be his children who had joined the company early on. As he thought back on it, Grace and Gavin came on board to help with one of the first big events. The two stepped in to help out with a couple of events, then never left. Overall, Grasshopper was pleased that his children had joined the company.

It gave him a sense of satisfaction to take a moment before an event to look out over the set tables and the busy staff, and to celebrate the company's accomplishments. Grace, Gavin, Gale, and Gus had all found places in his business. His spouse, Greg, enjoyed running the back end of the organization. They were so fortunate! The business was profitable. Grasshopper took a moment to acknowledge the gift of acceptance. The acceptance of a gay couple with a large family into the business community felt good. It was an acknowledgement of the skillset that both he and Greg brought to the table in the business, and in the community. Each person had their role and seemed happy.

Until that day at Jitterbug, Grasshopper had truly believed that his family was as happy as he was with the business as a family enterprise. It was a shock to discover that he was the only one who felt that sense of satisfaction. In fact, Grasshopper had felt blind-sided by the frustration Grace and Gavin unloaded that day. Both felt he had, once again, undermined their authority at an event. The other blow came when Greg weighed in and agreed with the kids. Whoa! That really hurt!

The experience taught him an important lesson. He had known that he needed to step back from the day-to-day operations of the business. Ant and Ms. Ladybug had brought his BIMBO tendencies to his attention for years. Grasshopper had set the intention to make addressing this limiting habit his number one priority for the year. He had started the year off by diving into sales, operations, and staffing to explore opportunities to develop, promote, and dele-gate his responsibilities in those areas.

He knew from the work he had done each year with Ant and Ms. Ladybug that his exit strategy was to grow the value of his busi-ness by acquiring other events companies, or strategic partners. This would make his company more valuable to prospective buyers as well as gain market share of the events business. In the event that his kids took over the business, well, they would have the space to advance through the different divisions.

Grasshopper hoped to create additional value with prospective buyers by empowering and delegating responsibility to his manage-ment team which included his children. He knew that this would also support his efforts to grow, by giving his banker additional confidence in the company as a stand-alone enterprise. Grasshopper believed that his intentions had been sound.

Grasshopper even had a plan for implementing the initiatives within Wingsong. He created goals with actionable steps. He then reviewed each with the relevant personnel. Grace, Gavin, and Greg were part of the decisions. He checked each initiative for alignment with his values and long-term plan. It all seemed to be aligned properly. As he began to execute the plans, his family seemed excited. The energy around the company was positive, and things were getting done.

Then, wedding season hit. They had had two bridezillas to satisfy, with large profits riding on each event. In hindsight, Grasshopper could see how he overreacted by stepping in and taking control at the Jitterbug event without leaving space for Grace and Gavin to step up. He now saw that his actions communicated a lack of trust in his children. It was a very public show of no faith, too. The staff, vendors, and customers at both events saw Grasshopper grab the reins from Grace and Gavin without thinking twice about it.

It was much too late for Grasshopper to repair the damage by the time he had his "come to Jesus" moment with his family. Of course, that awakening had come about in a very public way, too. Grace and Gavin had pulled him outside to the back of the venue, confronted him, and then stormed off. When Grasshopper had turned to go back in, he saw that a small group of the venue staff had taken their break at a picnic table not far from the discussion. By the looks on their faces, he knew every word of the conversation with his kids had been heard by the group. Not good. Not good at all!

After he sorted through his thoughts and apologized to all concerned, he was able to process his emotions. Grasshopper identified his fear of failure as the driver behind his BIMBO tendencies. He thought he knew this about himself. What Grasshopper hadn't figured out until much later was that he also had a need to be seen as "the Man." Grasshopper wanted his family to see him as the hero, and he wanted his employees to see him in that role, too.

Grasshopper admitted to himself that he wanted everyone to see him that way. The thing under it all was that Grasshopper believed that he was fundamentally flawed and needed to prove that he was good enough to be successful. Once Grasshopper took the time to process all of the emotions and thoughts that negatively impacted his family and his business, he knew he needed help. And, if Grasshopper wanted to make headway on this, he needed help quickly.

It wasn't all bad, however. That experience served to motivate Grasshopper to contact the business coach, Ms. Bee, for himself, the management team, and the family. Through his work with Ms. Bee, Grasshopper learned that Greg agreed with what Grace and Gavin had said to him. Grasshopper needed to mentor, coach, and teach others how to run the events. Others needed the chance to learn from him while he was still in the CEO seat.

Working with Ms. Bee, the past six months had brought the first real changes to the way Grasshopper worked within the company. He had transitioned into an advisory role for sales. Ms. Bee also worked with the family members who were part of the company. Through coaching, the management team had taken on renewed energy. There was excitement in the air, and he loved it!

Wingsong now had Gale as manager of sales. Gus was in charge of operations. With Ms. Bee's help, Grasshopper had learned how to look at the structure of the company through the lens of a prospective buyer. He saw that employing the family checked a number of boxes, but that bringing in non-related employees would make the company an overall stronger acquisition candidate.

So, they had hired someone from outside of the family to direct HR and manage seasonal staffing needs. The company's revenues were already climbing. Gale seemed to have a special talent for sales. She did a better job, and closed more sales at a higher price point than Grasshopper had in all of his years with the business. The company had surpassed its sales goals in September. The coming year should bring record profits for them. Grasshopper thought it was ironic. All this time he had hesitated to hand over certain tasks because he was convinced that no one could do them better than he did.

Grasshopper had rushed in to "fix" every problem for years, certain that no one cared as much as he did about customer satisfaction. How wrong he was on every front! Others could, and would, resolve any situation as well. It was very humbling. He felt like a fool. At the same time, he couldn't help but admit that it was also a huge relief. There were moments he felt stressed by the pressure of his old set of beliefs, with whispers in his mind about needing to be "large and in charge." Fortunately, with Ms. Bee's help he caught those limiting beliefs earlier. He had developed a plan to mitigate those beliefs, and it worked.

Grasshopper realized that the changes he made in his approach to the business cascaded down to his family, too. As Grasshopper recognized that his relationships with his employees and his family improved, he felt his confidence increase in his abilities to maintain his new work habits. He also acknowledged how his beliefs impacted the way he dealt with people. When he let go of having to prove himself to everyone, he felt more relaxed and less driven.

Grasshopper became a stronger leader in the organization and the family. He and Greg were working toward a true partnership. As Grasshopper integrated his new tools of leadership, he was able to see issues that came up at events not as problems, but as opportunities for Grace, Gavin, Gale, and Gus. They now had debriefs after each event to discuss what went right, improvements to be implemented in their systems and processes, and group assessments of the performance of each member of the team. These debriefs had the air of scientists working to discover new formulas for success. Grasshopper loved being a part of these meetings!

Yes, indeed, Grasshopper had made great strides since last year's strategic planning meeting. Ant and Ms. Ladybug knew of his work with Ms. Bee. At every accountability meeting, both had offered their feedback. Both had engaged Ms. Bee for themselves and found friendly satisfaction as Grasshopper's work with her progressed. So, Ms. Bee would facilitate today's meeting. The Grasshopper family had come to a major decision, and he wanted to spend time on it today. The family had decided to grow, and to continue to build value within the company, BUT they had decided to hold it as a family business for the foreseeable future. That was a big change from his original plan.

With another look at his watch, Grasshopper picked up the pace. He wanted to check in with the Jitterbug staff about their event prep before he went into the strategic planning meeting.

As Grasshopper made his way to the brewery, so did Ant. Grasshopper was not the only one deep in thought. Ant had had a very satisfying year. The business and the family had prospered. The accountability relationship with Grasshopper had continued to develop, and that warmed him. He felt such gratitude to both Grasshopper and Ms. Ladybug, who had continued to mentor both of them.

That thought surprised him. He gave a sheepish chuckle as Ant acknowledged to himself that he continued to discount Grasshopper's contributions to the relationship, despite evidence to the contrary. Not only had the weekly meetings continued, but Grasshopper had also made significant strides towards building value within his company.

The irony was Grasshopper's willingness to share his issues had allowed Ant to learn from those experiences. So, when Ant's children (or any other employee) appeared to be restless or disgruntled, he jumped on it immediately. Ant met with them individually or as a group as soon as he thought there might be a problem. In the past, he probably would've let it go. He didn't enjoy conflict and thought emotion had no place in a business. He now knew that emotions needed to be processed and managed to fully access logic and reasoning. He also admitted that avoidance was a business decision in and of itself. It was a decision that was often to the detriment of the company's culture and bottom line profits.

In the beginning, the meetings with the kids didn't appear to help. Ms. Bee encouraged him to hang in there and keep working on this. It helped a lot. It was one of the reasons Ant had encouraged Grasshopper to seek out Ms. Bee and work with her. It was once Grasshopper began working with Ms. Bee that Ant recognized the tools that she brought to the Grasshopper family business. She coached Grasshopper on facilitating those family meetings which helped a lot. So, when Ant met with her, he asked her to coach him through those types of meetings, too. Actually, he asked her to facilitate several of the family meetings and the team meetings, so that he could watch her in action. He had taken notes about what she said and why she said it in a particular way. It helped Ant develop his own approach.

Ant and the management team now took turns facilitating their meetings. There was an agenda with time allotted to celebrate wins, process opportunities for improvement, and discuss issues to generate options. The meetings were meaningful and efficient in that little time was spent rehashing "old issues." Time spent outside of the meetings was used to experiment and brainstorm, not complain about being heard or valued.

As Ant reached for an overview of Ant Hill Excavation, he realized that the team was capable of running the company without him. As long as the current players were in place, a prospective buyer could come in and run the company without a hitch. The weak link, however, was a lack of development of the next generation of management ("bench strength"). In the scenario that played on the possibility that one of his leaders became ill, or had some other type of emergency, Ant would have to step into that role, which was a problem. He needed to bring this to their attention and generate a plan to develop a process for identifying and hiring key talent.

Ant was excited that Ms. Bee would be the facilitator for this year's strategy session. He wanted to discuss this topic with Ms. Bee, Grasshopper, and Ms. Ladybug. He was looking forward to the energy of their brainstorming sessions and feedback. This was the first time that the three of them would be together to work on each of their businesses for a day with a business coach. Ant was so grateful that his team could handle the business for the day. He had looked forward to spending the time working ON his business, not just IN it.

The last item on Ant's agenda for the day was the change in his exit strategy, which tied into the learning and development plan for hiring to retain key leaders in the company. Ant's children were employed by the company. They were doing a great job, and every year they developed their own strategic plans. Several of the kids had expressed interest in owning their own companies. They had discussed buying smaller companies with the potential of becoming strategic partners for the excavation business. It was family business on a larger scale and could hold the key for creating generational wealth.

Also, Ant had fielded several more unsolicited calls from prospective buyers over the past year. He and the management team had discussed each inquiry. They explored the factors that created value for each interested buyer for Ant Hill Excavation. They looked at what might be advantageous for the family about an offer for the company. The team concluded that there might be more opportunities for Ant Hill Excavation as an acquirer than as an acquisition. This was the change from his initial strategy, and he really wanted Ms. Bee, Ms. Ladybug, and Grasshopper to weigh in on these thoughts.

Ant realized that he was also looking forward to the day because Grasshopper and Ms. Ladybug were his friends, as well as his mentors and accountability partners. He had a lot to be grateful for in his family, friends, and business. Life wasn't perfect, but it was really good right now.

Ms. Ladybug and Ms. Bee were getting settled in the space for the meeting today. Ms. Ladybug took a moment to thank Ms. Bee for her willingness to act as a thought partner, transformational agent, and driver for growth and development. Ms. Bee accepted the thanks and pointed out that Ms. Ladybug did the work willingly. Ms. Ladybug knew that was true, but she also felt that gratitude all the way down to her red and black toes.

Ms. Ladybug leaned close and whispered, "Can we take a minute so that I can share something with the group before we begin the strategy session? I'd really appreciate it."

"Of course, Ms. Ladybug! Not a problem!" said Ms. Bee. "This is the time to share and learn."

Both turned to greet Ant as he entered the room. Ms. Ladybug asked him, "How are you?" Ant nodded at both as he placed his bag down on the table. "I'm great, thank you! It's so good to see the two of you. I am looking forward to our discussions today. Anybody seen Grasshopper yet?"

The three exchanged smiles and looks that each understood to mean that Grasshopper had stayed true to form. He was late.

About twenty minutes later, Grasshopper entered the room. "Hey, how are you all? I can't wait to get started! I have so much to tell you."

Ant, who couldn't let this pass by, responded with, "Good of you to attend. Did you forget where we were to meet? You're late!"

"No, I wasn't late. I've been here for an hour. I just wasn't in here." Grasshopper looked pleased. "I was actually early for a change!"

"You know, it doesn't count as early if you're in the building, but late to the actual meeting. What were you doing if you weren't in here waiting for us?" asked Ms. Ladybug.

"My company has an event here in a few days. The set up has started, and the guys here wanted me to be on hand to answer a few questions. Today I am following Eisenhower's Matrix for Time Management by being here at Jitterbug for the important and urgent tasks of the day. And, as I just happened to score this site for our meeting, it also covers the important, but not urgent, strategic planning meeting as well. Isn't that great?" Grasshopper beamed his special smile and appeared to be extraordinarily pleased with himself.

Ms. Bee turned to Ms. Ladybug and said, "I know that you wanted to start us off, but I'm going to ask you to let me do so. Sound okay to you?" Ms. Ladybug nodded. "Okay then. Grasshopper, you and I have spent a considerable amount of time working on what issues?"

"Mostly things connected to the BIMBO syndrome. Building an

empowered team, limiting my hands-on moments during a crisis, and letting others learn through their mistakes. Basically, setting up the business to be valuable to a prospective buyer." Grasshopper sat back and crossed his arms over his chest. "I believe I've done some great work here."

"You have, Grasshopper, you have," replied Ms. Bee. "It's why I want to bring this to your attention. You have set goals, gathered new tools, and implemented new practices to ensure that you build value in the company. What I want to challenge you on here is this notion of being efficient. How efficient is this to be on call for the set up crew, while you are here to focus on your strategic plan for next year?"

"Oh, well, uh. Hmmm, I'm not sure. I guess we can wait and see," replied Grasshopper.

"Grasshopper, I have an idea. Take it or leave it, there is no pressure to try this at all. How about you make a mark with a time annotation for every time you are interrupted by the Jitterbug staff during our meeting? How would you feel about doing that and then taking a look at it at the end of the day?" asked Ms. Bee.

"Sure, I can totally do that, Ms. Bee. It's just that I didn't want to miss the meeting today. And, I felt like being on call for the set up crew was also important. I thought this was the perfect solution," said Grasshopper.

"I can see that from your perspective, Grasshopper, it would make sense. What I'm curious about is whether that makes sense from the perspective of a business owner who feels like the business is their baby, or from a CEO mindset. I'd also like to find out what impact this arrangement has on your ability to focus and concentrate throughout the day. How about it? Are you up for the experiment?" Ms. Bee looked at him pointedly.

"Yes, I'm willing to do it. Thanks for bringing this to my attention, Ms. Bee." Grasshopper sat up straight and uncrossed his arms.

Ms. Bee turned to Ms. Ladybug and invited her to begin.

"Thanks, Ms. Bee." Ms. Ladybug turned to Ant and Grasshopper. "I think I told the two of you a few weeks ago about my college reunion. I had so much fun seeing my friends and reliving old times. I expected that would be my main takeaway. What I didn't expect was to rediscover people who weren't friends then that are now so interesting twenty-five years later." Ladybug laughed. "We are sometimes so arrogant when we're young, aren't we? Anyway, I got to talking with an acquaintance who is a climatologist. She has developed a climate preparedness tool for companies to use as an assessment of not only the risk to their businesses but also the opportunities associated with climate change. The conversation is still playing in my head."

With a frown, Ant asked Ms. Ladybug, "How is this important to us? We don't live on the coasts. We don't experience severe droughts or hurricanes. I don't see how our companies are under any threat or have any opportunities on the horizon from climate change."

Grasshopper laughed, "Was that pun intentional, Ant? That's a good one... on the horizon! I like that." Grasshopper turned to Ms. Ladybug, "But I agree with Ant. How is this a good use of our time?" Just then a light tap drew their attention to the doorway. It was someone from the set-up crew. The guy indicated that he needed Grasshopper for "just a sec."

Ms. Bee looked at Grasshopper and made a tally mark gesture. "First of many?" Then, she turned to Ant and Ms. Ladybug, "Please continue, Ms. Ladybug. I'd like to hear more."

Ms. Ladybug nodded, "As I said, I've just started to consider this issue. You all know that I've struggled to hire skilled labor and fear that the shortage is going to continue. I've taken steps to hire people willing to learn, and I've developed programs to teach the required skills, while also focusing on values and a strong work ethic as other essential criteria for the hire. So, what if a critical mass of my workforce is from a country that is devastated by a climate event? Will they stay or feel obligated to return to their native country to rebuild there? I've not asked my workers where they are from as it seemed like an intrusion on their privacy in our current political environment."

Ms. Ladybug took a deep breath and continued. "What that climatologist brought to my attention in just a couple of minutes of conversation were a few scenarios:

1. Suppose the temperature continues to rise each year. In five years, that steady rise could impact my employees' abilities to be out in the heat during the summer building houses. That rise in temperature would likely affect the integrity of HVAC equipment and installation, along with rough-ins like plumbing and electricity. We would need to schedule more frequent breaks, supply more electrolyte beverages like Sqwincher, and inspect the seals and any other connections that may be affected by heat. We could also experience more frequent brownouts by the power company during peak demand.

2. A climate event in another area of the country could affect our ability to build new houses for our current residents, but suppose we experience another migration of evacuees like we did after Hurricane Katrina? What role will my company play in a scenario like that? I wonder if that would become an opportunity for growth.

3. The last scenario had not occurred to me either. If the weather patterns shift, and the severe storms of the past few years become standard here, how can I adjust our methods of building so that one of those storms doesn't put us back on every job we have in process? This last one is a challenge. You might remember that last summer we had three houses going up when that big storm came through. We lost two generators to theft, and it took two days to restore the framing to pre-storm conditions. The third house lost its roof's base and the exterior sheathing. It was an expensive mess that actually could have been much worse.

The long and short of it is that I no longer feel comfortable just hoping for better weather. The stats indicate that weather is going to be a consideration for all of us in one way or another. We have always acted preemptively. I'd like for us to spend some time on this issue today. I don't think we can completely solve anything here, but I'd like to think about the risks and the opportunities with all of you."

Just then, Grasshopper returned to the room. "I'm back! What did I miss? Anything big?" Ms. Ladybug sighed, leaned back, and repeated what she had just shared. "I'd like for us to devote some time to this topic today. Are you good with that, Grasshopper?" asked Ms. Ladybug.

"Of course, Ms. Ladybug. What would happen to me if those storms became common? I was fortunate that none of the storms happened during one of my events. Also, I depend on vendors and the beauty of venues. A serious storm could disrupt deliveries and destroy the venues. That could be catastrophic to my business."

Just then, Ms. Bee picked up her head and spoke to Grasshopper, "You have just used the word 'my' to describe the events. I'm going to suggest using either 'our' or 'the' to create additional separation between your identity and the business. How does that sound to you, Grasshopper?"

"What is this, pick on Grasshopper day? I'm getting the feeling that I still have a lot of work to do to leave my BIMBO tendencies behind, don't I? Yes, Ms. Bee, in addition to keeping track of the number of times I'm interrupted by the set up crew, I will also make an effort to separate myself from Wingsong in my mind. Ms. Bee, I am so glad that you are my coach, but I have to tell you the energy in this meeting has changed drastically just by having you here with us. Do you plan to challenge me all day today? I don't know if I can take it!" Grasshopper looked around and then stopped when he came to Ms. Bee.

Ms. Bee smiled and nodded. "Grasshopper, that observation is very insightful about the changes in the meeting. Whenever we introduce someone new into a room, the energy is different. You've invited me here to facilitate. Part of my role is to challenge the existing patterns — not necessarily to change them, but to expand your awareness around those patterns. For example, you have hired me to work with you as you and your family create a business that is sustainable. You have recognized that the value of a business increases when the business is a separate entity from the owner. That is what will appeal to an investor or a prospective buyer. It also leaves the CEO free to focus on forecasting, planning for the unexpected, and strategizing. Other advantages of this approach are an empowered management team and a healthier CEO."

"I know, I know. You are so right, Ms. Bee. I have a long way to go. Two steps forward, one step back. Thank you all for being patient with my efforts to grow into a CEO." After this speech, Grasshopper shook his head ruefully. He wondered if he would ever get this right. Then, a thought occurred to Grasshopper. He jumped up and asked, "Can we take a five-minute break? I want to make a quick call."

The others glanced at one another and then back at Grasshopper. "Sure. Let's break for ten minutes and warm up our coffee. Then, we can come back and focus on the agenda we set for today," said Ms. Bee.

During the break, they saw Grasshopper make his call. He then had a quick conversation with the set up crew. When Ant, Ms. Ladybug, and Ms. Bee returned to the room, Grasshopper was already in place with his materials in front of him, along with a steaming mug of java.

Ant asked Grasshopper, "What was that all about?"

"Well," said Grasshopper, "I realized that Ms. Bee was spot-on in her assessment of my abilities to concentrate in here while the set up was going on in the event space. My attention was divided between the two. I know myself well enough that I can't totally focus on our time here if I think I might be needed out there. So, I called Grace to ask if one of the team could come out here to be the point of contact for the set up crew. It wasn't a problem. Gail and Gus are on their way here. This is their event, and they are the logical choices to be here. It never occurred to me to do this until

Ms. Bee called me out on my initial plan. Like I said, I have a long way to go to be a dedicated CEO and not just another hands-on manager."

"Well done, Grasshopper! No need to keep track of interruptions. You are on your way to making the most of this time together," said Ms. Ladybug. She turned to Ms. Bee. "Ms. Bee, let's get this party started!"

The four turned their attention to their agenda, adding a discussion about climate contingency planning when they ran scenarios. The end of the day brought the discussions to a close. Grasshopper and Ms. Bee led the discussions on communication, especially the importance of buy-in from key stakeholders within the family and the company. Ms. Ladybug was pleased that the climate preparedness discussion had led to two new ideas for her team to develop in the coming year. Ant had a full agenda for the coming year that included expansion and meetings with his financial advisor to determine how much he could invest in his children's new companies.

"Whew, what a long day! My head is so full, I can hardly contain it all," exclaimed Grasshopper.

"Same here. This next year will fly by just like the last eight years have passed. You know, we are so fortunate to have one another. I know that I'm supposed to be your mentor, but I have to tell you that I learn as much from you as you learn from me. At this point, I feel we are peers. I am so grateful you asked me to mentor you. I'm convinced that I've learned more by being a mentor than you have being mentored. I'm curious how the two of you feel about our working together?" Ms. Ladybug put both elbows on the table and leaned in to look at Ant and Grasshopper.

Ant spoke up first. "I have learned so much from the two of you. You have challenged me. Both of you supported me as I've navigated the family ties alongside the business demands. I'm still floored by the growth of Ant Hill Excavation and amazed by the aspirations that my children now have. I believe that you both have contributed to my growth as a husband, father, and the company. I didn't dare to hope that the company could be so profitable in such a short period of time."

Ant continued by pointing out, "And you both know that when we first talked about exit strategies, I thought it was a waste of time. Granted, that plan has changed each year, but so has my attitude about exit planning. Now the plan is more organic, leading to greater flexibility depending on the market as well as on the management team. Lastly, I'm not sure I'd have been able to identify the weaknesses in my hiring strategy or the lack of a plan for learning and development of potential leaders within the organization. I also have to thank you, Grasshopper, for sharing your experiences. Ms. Ladybug, I'm so grateful to you for introducing us to Mr. Walking Stick, Ms. Butterfly as well as Ms. Bee. You both have become friends in addition to colleagues, and I want to thank you for that, too." Then, Ant gave them both a sweet smile that warmed their hearts.

"Well, it's my turn." As he spoke, Grasshopper shifted in his seat. "I'm so grateful to the two of you. I feel like we're all friends, too, although there are many times I feel like the two of you are way ahead of me in development. Ms. Ladybug, I appreciate your mentorship. Ant, I cannot begin to express how grateful I am that you agreed to be my accountability buddy. If not for the two of you, I'm certain I'd already be out of business, and probably divorced."

Grasshopper sighed and then went on. "I agree with all that you both have said. I'd like to add that the yearly planning meetings have been so important. As you both know, I struggle with getting lost in the day-to-day operations. Yes, yes, BIMBO syndrome here." Grasshopper acknowledged their smiles. "What I'm saying is that I'm aware of my BIMBO tendencies. These yearly planning meetings allow me to see the impact in real time. The yearly meetings also force me to confront the progress or lack of progress, towards creating a standalone company."

He continued by saying, "My exit strategy has changed, too, over time. My company, Wingsong Events, is still not an appealing investment opportunity due to my ongoing involvement. However, by working with Ms. Bee, I believe I'll make real progress on that this year. I wish I had started work with her sooner. But I know I'll get there faster working with her than I would without her. With Ms. Bee and the two of you, I am a stronger leader and father, too. I know I'm a better person because of these relationships. Not to mention, neither of us has had to go hungry a single winter since we started our businesses. That's a win in every way!"

The day closed out with Ms. Bee leading a discussion on the major takeaways for the day, as well as their identified obstacles to success. Ant, Grasshopper, and Ms. Ladybug summarized their goals, action steps, and tools on one sheet of paper to take back to their teams. It was a day well spent!

And the Moral of the Story is... *To paraphrase hockey great Wayne Gretzky, Hop to where the puck is going to be, not where it has been.*

Planning is a vital form of preparation. Planning is also a process of discovery. You learn where your blind spots are, how your knowledge gaps might derail your goals, and what tools you may need to develop for success. Know that you can ask for help. You are never expected to know everything.

Recently, we had the opportunity to conduct a day-long workshop with a group of business owners. We debriefed the past year, looked at what worked, didn't work, and needed to change. Each participant identified systems and processes that had contributed to their success, as well as things that needed to change to make room for success.

One owner made the following connections:

1. In reviewing last year's performance, the company had $3 million in submitted, yet denied or lost, proposals. The owner realized that the one salesperson the

company had on the team was underpaid. The salesperson was paid according to what the owner felt comfortable with paying. (Money story alert! It was a nice, safe number.) Yet, if the owner had paid the salesperson a percentage of the booked sales, it's possible that more contracts would have been awarded. Interesting, isn't it?

2. Another owner, like Grasshopper, realized that time spent on a new venture could be delegated. The owner could oversee the project and delegate the more detail-oriented tasks to staff. This owner wasn't ready to commit to the new venture and thought it best to keep it on the down-low. However, the value of time versus the value of secrecy did not add up. It made sense to use staff to complete some of the necessary tasks than for the owner to try to accomplish everything.

3. Every attendee of the workshop walked away feeling as though the day wasn't long enough. Each feedback form requested more time next year, along with suggestions for additional experts as guest speakers.

Reader, how much time do you devote to debriefing, planning, and goal setting? How about worst- and best-case scenario planning? Who runs your sessions, if in fact you have them? How would you feel about taking a page from our friends' playbook and allowing your team to take turns facilitating? How would you feel about hiring a business coach to facilitate your annual meeting and planning sessions?

If you are unsure of the benefits of such meetings, then we strongly encourage you to consider hiring a facilitator. Meaningful meetings are important. Wasteful meetings drain the team's energy and negatively impact the team's ability to successfully achieve their goals.

Consider using the agenda template provided at the end of this section for your next planning meeting. You can send it out to the team in advance to stimulate their thoughts on each topic. For those of you in family businesses or companies with a family culture, you have a responsibility to set aside time to discuss the sticky, messy topics that come up during the year. Ignoring those subjects year after year can erode the company from the inside, impacting profits as well as culture.

As you recall, Grasshopper described a painful confrontation that happened during an event with his children. He knew he stepped on toes and undermined those he placed in charge of each event. It's a challenge for every parent to learn to parent. It's like flying a plane while you are still building it, isn't it? Grasshopper and Ant are not alone in their struggles to be successful financially while trying to be parents to adult children and the employers of those same adult children. It's complicated!

If these are the kinds of topics that you are reluctant to discuss openly and authentically, then you are not alone, and you need help. Think about it. When was the last time you asked for help? How far into the situation were you before you decided to ask for help? We'd love to know the internal narrative that ran through your mind during that time.

We've had a number of clients who were unaware that they believed that asking for help was a sign of weakness or failure. Once they acknowledged the fallacy of those beliefs, each success-fully learned new tools to eliminate those limiting beliefs and make way for the truth. Clearing out those beliefs gives you the mental capacity to seek out the people who can help you fill your knowl-edge gaps, expose your blind spots, and navigate any difficult conversation with integrity. Think about the most successful people that you know. Do they have at least some of these best practices?

Our list of successful people includes three people who publicly acknowledged that part of their success was due to a trust-worthy second, or partner. Sir Edmund Hillary and his partner, Tenzing Norgay, were the first to scale Mt. Everest. Warren Buffet and Charlie Munger have been partners of the successful holding company, Berkshire Hathaway, for sixty years. Player Tom Brady and Coach Bill Belichick reaped the benefits of a highly successful working relationship with the NFL team, the New England Patriots, that spanned almost twenty years. Each of these dynamic duos spent years working alongside one another. They didn't always agree. They chose to always listen to the other person. Each pair learned from one another.

Each of these people were lifelong learners. They listened, honestly disagreed, and continued to benefit from their willingness to learn from the other's experiences, while admitting that they didn't have all of the answers. This approach is used by the characters in our fable. It's also the approach we encourage our clients to use with their families and teams. A business coach is a great way to gain the benefits of a partnership without the financial commitment of hiring another employee.

Our characters covered a lot of ground in this chapter. Each brought issues that they worked on throughout the year to their yearly strategy meeting. We believe that there is wisdom in following some, if not all, of these practices today. Here is a summary:

1. Journal about your challenges.
2. Give time and attention to difficult conversations.
3. Consider the people in your life that can act as your thought partners. If you don't have anyone who has the requisite skills and will maintain your confidentiality, hire a business coach.
4. Identify your limiting beliefs. Know where they appear in your life and in your business.

It is never weak to ask for help. No one is expected to have every answer. Go ahead, ask. You will go much further much faster with help than you ever would alone.

Many business owners feel overwhelmed, tired, and stressed. Shortages of time and money are commonly used by business owners as the basis for decisions to put off planning, to not hire the external advisors that could fill their knowledge gaps, and to avoid empowering team members. It may be easier for the business owner and the team to stay in the here and now, avoiding the future. However, by refusing to prioritize planning tied to company mission, values, and purpose, the owner abdicates responsibility in creating a company that is built to last for generations to come.

Use this sample agenda, "Tune to Success," to guide you and your team in planning for the future. Modify it for your industry and company. Make this part of your planning portfolio — bring this out and use it quarterly.

Businesses that are healthy, financially sound, and culturally tied to mission and purpose allow those who work in those businesses to live the fullest, most authentic lives. The infographic that follows the sample agenda highlights skills that translate those used in business to leadership skills used in our personal lives. Both PDFs are available at www.ascendcoachingsolutions.com for download.

TUNE TO SUCCESS

ALIGN   VALUES, MISSION, PURPOSE, VISION

Goals & Timelines for next decade (from last year)

SHARE   GOALS WITH TACTICS & ACTION STEPS

Add to timeline - steps taken, goals to be achieved, proposals, innovations, opportunities, trends

CREATE   PLAN, PRACTICE READINESS

Run scenarios for disruptions, weather interruptions, catastrophic illness of key people, death, unsolicited offers or inquiries, exit strategies for key stakeholders

ESTABLISH   EXIT STRATEGIES

Unsolicited offers or inquiries, exit strategies for key stakeholders, desired outcomes, ideal prospects

NAVIGATE   BUILD RESILIENCE

Empower the team - establish psychological safety in which every voice is heard. Design learning and experience goals for leadership development. Curate the learning from all risk, using a growth mindset.

DISCERN   SWOT ANALYSIS

Conduct the SWOT analysis as a team. Discuss 360 reviews through the lens of curiosity. What does each team member need to succeed? What does the company need to succeed?

THE BUSINESS OF LIVING A FULL LIFE

1 LEADERSHIP PRINCIPLES @HOME
Lead through, adapting to, the debrief that follows the change. Curate learning. Model vulnerability & transparency.

2 BE THE CEO OF THE LEGACY OF YOU
Invest in your strengths & gifts. Use a growth mindset. Identify your blind spots & knowledge gaps. Connect & fill.

3 ACCEPT REALITY - BE AUTHENTIC
Your are who you are - despite the wishes & pressures of society. You are enough. Develop the courage to be you.

4 ENVISION YOUR FUTURE
Explore ways to improve your health, emotional, spiritual, intellectual, social, & environmental well-being to be ready!

ASCEND COACHING SOLUTIONS

BETTER LIFE, BETTER BUSINESS COACHING
WWW.ASCENDCOACHINGSOLUTIONS.COM

CELEBRATE THE FRUITS OF YOUR LABOR!

Fun Fact: Ants constructing an average-sized mound carry 88 tons of soil to the surface.

I t was a beautiful autumn day in the forest. The sun was shining, and the breeze had a touch of chill. The leaves had turned brilliant shades of red, gold, and orange. Winter was coming soon, and Grasshopper could not have cared any less.

Grasshopper was on his way to meet his old friends, Ant and Ladybug, to play a celebratory round of golf. The three friends, colleagues, and accountability partners had a lot to celebrate!

"It happened! It really happened!" Grasshopper couldn't help shouting out loud. He tilted his head back and yelled to the tree-tops, "I did it! We all did it! No more hungry winters! We did it!" and he took a giant leap into the air.

Ahead on the path, Grasshopper saw Ant, who was laughing hard. It was an amazing sight to see Ant with his head thrown back, laughing out loud. Grasshopper came up to Ant with a big smile on his face. "You saw that, did you, Ant?" asked Grasshopper.

Ant then bent over laughing even harder. The two stood there together on the path, laughing like crazy. After a while, Ant straightened up and spoke with some difficulty, "Yes, I did, Grasshopper. It's a great feeling, isn't it? We actually brought our crazy dreams to life." He took another steadying breath. "Come on, let's get to the course because Ms. Ladybug is waiting for us. She's an important part of this celebration, and here we are starting without her." The two hurried on to meet Ladybug, both chatting about their new next chapter in life.

Ladybug was standing just inside the clubhouse door. She waited eagerly for her old friends. Ladybug was so excited to have an entire morning to talk to Ant, Bee, and Grasshopper about what was next for all of them. As she peered around looking for her friends, someone called her name.

Looking over, she saw Walking Stick. "Good morning, Ms. Ladybug!" he called out. "Good morning, Walking Stick!" said Ladybug.

"Have you recovered from the sale of your company?" asked Walking Stick. She shook her head. "How does it feel to be here instead of walking a job site or stuck in your office on a beautiful day?" He smiled as he asked the question.

"It feels really good and really strange. It's fun to see you today. I'm meeting Bee, Ant, and Grasshopper here. We planned this not only to celebrate, but also to process all that has happened during the last year. I think you know that while I sold my business, Ant and Grasshopper 'passed the torch' to their families. The three of us handed over our CEO hats at about the same time." Ladybug smiled as she caught sight of Grasshopper and Ant walking toward the entrance.

Ladybug smiled at Walking Stick and spoke. "You and Butterfly were a huge help. I'm so glad that the two of you came to that strategy planning day years ago. That was the beginning of the real exit planning for the three of us."

Ladybug teared up a little and then regained her composure as she started speaking again. "Both of you gave us the opportunity to look at our companies from the eyes of an investor or a buyer. We needed the relationships we built with the two of you over the years. The two of you and Bee reminded us of what was important to make our dreams come true." Just then, Ant and Grasshopper entered and hurried over to Ladybug and Walking Stick.

Grasshopper reached out to embrace both of them as he said, "Well, well. How fitting to have you here at this moment, Walking Stick! I understand you were at the table when Ms. Ladybug sold her business. Congratulations are in order, I see."

Ant then leaned forward to hug Ladybug, while reaching out with another hand to shake with Walking Stick. He said, "Yes! Congratulations, Walking Stick! Well done!" He then turned to Ladybug, "How are you, Ms. Ladybug? You look like you are doing well."

"I couldn't be better! May I say that the two of you also look refreshed and relaxed. I'm not sure I've ever seen either of you look so rested. How do you feel? Any regrets?" Ladybug laughed as she asked and looked at both of her friends with fondness.

As if it were choreographed, the four turned as each became

aware of Bee. She stood there, looking at them with a huge smile on her face. She laughed as she said, "What an amazing day! You do look happy and relaxed, but also a bit dazed."

Grasshopper straightened, "Oh my gosh, this is great, are you joining us? That would be so cool!"

Bee answered, "Yes, Ms. Ladybug and Ant invited me to join in and help debrief. Of course, we also have to celebrate the rewards of the years of hard work by the three of you."

"I'd also like to encourage each of you to come up with at least one actionable step to make the next chapter of your lives even more successful by the end of our time together today," said Bee. Grasshopper made a face, and they all laughed at his resistance for one last step, as he already appeared to have fully embraced his new retirement lifestyle.

Bee continued beaming at the group, even Grasshopper. "The skills you used to create successful, profitable, valuable businesses need translation to be applied to retirement, or to the role of the 'wise sage' for others. That's why I'd like for you to think about one next step before you leave today. You know, something to use as a launch point to get each of you started."

Walking Stick offered another round of handshakes and congratulations, then took his leave. The four made their way out of the clubhouse to begin their round of golf.

As they settled into the game, Grasshopper noted with a glum expression, "I think this is going to be a very long morning. I told you that I don't play golf. I'm not any good at it."

Bee turned to him with a twinkle in her eyes and said, "Grasshopper, you've never played golf before. You told us that this was your first time. You have just played your very first hole! How could you possibly be good at this?"

Ant spoke up, "She's right. You might remember that Bee encouraged us to start investing some time in new interests or hobbies a few years ago. I thought I might like it, so I took some lessons. This game is a lot harder than it looks on ESPN." He laughed and nodded his head.

"I know that I saw the pros walk out onto a beautiful green, have some other guy hand them a club, gently hit the ball into the hole, and walk off to applause. Ha! I was so wrong! I took lessons for a year. After one month, I realized it was a game that took skill and a ton of practice. I liked it fine but didn't have the time to devote to it. I've taken a lesson a month since that time and am looking forward to finally getting better at it."

"Ant and Bee are right, Grasshopper," chimed in Ladybug. "I felt like the best construction contracts were awarded on the golf course. So, a number of years ago, I took lessons and began a half-hearted attempt to play. I played well enough to get by, but I didn't land any contracts. No one wanted to play a round with me. I was always holding up the game. It's a lot harder than it looks. Other than our game today, I don't play as a rule. I don't enjoy playing with anyone who is super competitive." She grinned. "As a matter of fact, I wouldn't have agreed to play today, except I knew that you'd not played before, so I'd probably be okay."

Grasshopper looked at her sideways and grinned. "Okay, in other words, as long as you come out ahead of me, you'll be good. Right?"

Ladybug laughed, "Right!"

Bee spoke up. "Let's focus on what just happened here. I believe it's relevant for our discussion on who you will each be in your next phase of life. Grasshopper, what do you know about yourself?"

Grasshopper's brow furrowed as he thought. Suddenly he seemed to get it, as his expression cleared and he answered, "I'm impulsive. I live in the moment without a lot of energy going into the future. I want the results. Ha! I also tend not to be introspective, so I don't spend energy on the past."

He continued, "In my business, these tendencies helped me show up to every appointment totally focused in the moment. I was able to solve problems with ease. Crises didn't get to me. I liked it, so a lot of times I may have actually created havoc without even knowing it. I thrived on the chaos. Those same tendencies also hurt my business at times. I had to learn to be a leader and to plan, strategize, and execute within the team, as part of the team. That took a long time. I wanted the results without doing the work. Kinda like golf, I guess." Grasshopper grinned sheepishly.

Bee nodded and then spoke, "So, knowing all of that, what can you do to set yourself up to successfully navigate the transition from CEO to 'wise sage' within your family governance? When I say 'governance,' I'm talking about making sure everyone in your family feels comfortable in the roles they are in and ensuring they lead in their new roles within the business."

Grasshopper pondered Bee's words, "Well, I can continue to work on expanding my self-awareness. I can invite those around me to offer feedback and observations on those patterns of behavior. I also intend to continue to work with you, Bee, on this transition. Believe me, I have learned my lesson on blustering and bullying my family members, as well as the team. I am practicing radical transparency even when I am shaking in my boots to hear what others think of my behaviors. My goals are to develop a couple of passion projects, things I can work on that I've always wanted to do but didn't because of my business. I want my next phase to be as productive as my last."

Bee nodded again and then offered, "Grasshopper, look how far you have come! You achieved your goal of positioning your business as a valuable asset. You've established a team of people to take the business to the next level. You recognized that you were no longer the person best suited to lead the company through that next stage. You did the work and reaped the rewards."

She continued, "Today, what I'd like to hear from each of you is one action step that you are committed to taking in the next month. What step can you take that will move you toward those goals around your passion projects?"

Grasshopper bowed his head as he thought. "I'd like to think about that during this next hole. But first, let me share with you what my passions are. First, I'd like to get back to making music. As you all know, that is my first love. Next, I want to see if any of my old friends are interested in starting a band. Last, I'd love to help prepare my grandkids for business by giving them opportunities to build strong relationships with other members of the family. That ought to keep me occupied for a good long while. I envision a lot of jamming and fishing with the kids." He laughed and looked at each of his friends.

The four friends spent the next few holes on the course discussing the struggles in closing Ladybug's sale. It was complicated as initially the highest bidders weren't interested in the training programs she had developed. It took some time before Ladybug and her team were able to communicate the connection between the training and the low rate of employee turnover in the company. Next, they tried to renegotiate the purchase price because they did not want to honor the standard practice of tossing out the period of time that impacted all businesses due to the pandemic.

Then, the highest bidder backed out over honoring the current service agreements and maintaining the prices for at least a year after closing. They then had to go back to the other interested parties. It took a dedicated team of Walking Stick, Butterfly, and Ladybug's management team to choose their next potential buyer. The second time around, Ladybug wasn't swayed as much by the purchase price as she was with the fit with her company's values, goals, and purpose.

"You know, Ms. Ladybug," said Bee, "I believe that that first buyer was great practice. Don't get me wrong, I know that was painful and expensive. It was also stressful. However, you learned the importance of self-care for yourself and your team. It also gave you the chance to gain clarity around what was really important for you as far as the outcome. Let me ask you this, how important was purchase price the first time as opposed to the second time?"

Ladybug's eyes seemed to lose focus for a few moments before she replied. "Well, the purchase price was huge with that first buyer. It was so disappointing that it didn't work out. But, with hindsight, I can honestly say I am so grateful that it didn't."

She sighed heavily. "It was, in fact, stressful and expensive and very painful. I felt so foolish and ashamed. At one point, I was so focused on not being ashamed anymore that I would have agreed to almost anything to make the situation go away. If it hadn't been for Bee and the management team to think that situation through with me, it could have been so much worse!"

Then Ladybug smiled. "Fortunately, I really did have a do-over. Since the first prospect backed out, thank goodness, it was easy to see that the other buyers really were a better fit for my goals. You know, I wanted to do everything I could to protect my management team and my employees. One of the cool things about the training programs was that our employees who were hurt, or no longer able to work in the field, could act as instructors. It was a great system for retaining our best personnel, as well as for developing new talent. That system created loyalty and saved us money because we didn't have to constantly replace employees. Also, we wanted to maintain the online training to be ready for any kind of disruption, like the pandemic that happened a while back.

"My other big consideration was the community. You all know our rate of growth over the past few years. Of course, the company contributes to the economy, but so do our employees. Their families rely on the income. Our people are confident in their ability to pay their bills and provide opportunities for their families, so they are willing to help out at the company and in the community whenever there is a need. That was to be my legacy, and I wanted that to be honored by the next owner," explained Ladybug.

She continued, "Once Bee and I worked on my priorities and desired outcomes, and revisited my values, I was able to rediscover my clarity and focus. Whew! When I think about what might have happened with that first buyer, I shudder. And I know that there are no guarantees with the new owner. But I've done all I can to set the company up to succeed for the future. I'm happy and ready to move on."

The four continued to work through the course. No one was in a hurry. They all remarked on the strangeness of the lack of urgency as they talked. Bee never let an opportunity pass that could be a coaching moment. Her questions made them think. They challenged one another and brainstormed action steps. During the conversation, Grasshopper learned that both Ant and Ladybug had engaged Bee to coach them through their transitions to retirement, too.

Ladybug laughed as Grasshopper attempted to nail down the details of the contract with Bee, who put a stop to that by saying, "You know how this works. We sit down, discuss your goals, and sign the contract. We know we work well together, so that won't be a part of the discussion. Once we finish here, let's schedule a meeting." Grasshopper readily agreed.

Then Bee turned to Ant and asked, "How about you, Ant? How are you feeling?"

Ant nodded and looked at each of his friends and colleagues. "I'm good. I feel like the weight of the world has been lifted from my shoulders. I visited the office one day last week. I had not finished cleaning out and moving my office. The team agreed with me that it is best that I keep a lower profile at the company. I have a home office that will allow me to work from there. There is such freedom in saying that! My new office at the company is smaller, just down the hall from Gavin's CEO office. It's tucked away in the corner with its own entrance. I can come and go as I please without reporting to anyone, and no one has the opportunity to report me missing. I love this!"

"Hmmm," Bee pondered as she tilted her head towards Ant. "What can you tell us about your new role within the team? How is that going?"

"Well, you coached me through that one, so I'd say it's going really well. The management team is set up to identify, process, and strategize for whatever initiatives the company has set. Gavin, as CEO, has his executive leadership team to determine what those initiatives will be for the company, with input from the management team, as well as from any other person in the company. Scenario planning is now a part of the process and culture. I believe Ant Hill Excavation is ready for anything with a resilience track record to prove it."

He paused briefly as he looked over to his old friend. "Grasshopper, you mentioned practicing radical transparency. Well, we count that practice as one of ours, too. In addition, we've tried to take the hierarchy out of the company structure. We have fewer 'big bosses,' and instead we've replaced them with a much flatter, team-oriented structure. It seems to be working as well now as it ever did with me at the helm in the past.

"I've gotta tell you all, I'm still surprised that the kids wanted to take over. I had operated for years as though we would sell. However, as those that wanted to work in the company found their places, the others seemed to identify other gaps to fill in terms of what the company needed or offered. They opted to fill those gaps with their own companies. It's gone amazingly well. We now function with a family council, a family assembly, and a family constitution. We have worked with Bee to set those things up with the appropriate external advisors." Ant looked up at the sky for a moment and then continued.

"We've even brought in management from outside of the company. We've promoted from within, and as a result, have identified several non-family members who show great promise. We've invested in those employees with additional training and coaching, as well as shown them a path for advancement that isn't dependent on family relationships. I believe it's not only sustainable, but it also increases the capacity of the company to grow well into the future." Ant looked over at Bee.

"I can't thank you enough for your work with us, and with me, over the last several years. I'm looking forward to the future with as much enthusiasm as Ms. Ladybug and Grasshopper — with you as my thought partner." Ant shrugged, "I thought retirement was for old people, and I dreaded it for a long time. Now, I've done a 180-degree turn. I'm filled with hope and anticipation, thanks to all of you." Ant gave a nod and picked up the club. "Let's get this done so that we can go to the clubhouse for lunch and a beer."

The game came to an end. The four made their way to the clubhouse where they ordered their beverage of choice and lunch. Bee cleared her throat and raised her glass of wine. "To the ultimate business owner experience! Assets, values, and identities intact! Cheers!" There were murmurs of "Yesssss!" and "Hurray!" along with the clink of glasses.

Bee then said, "I'd like for the three of you to consider continuing your accountability meetings and year-end strategy sessions. You are talented, energetic, and insightful individuals. You all have a lot of potential and can contribute a great deal to our community. Working alongside one another, you have accomplished great things. Your awareness of the need for accountability, as well as your need to learn from one another, brought you together. Transitioning to a role as an advisor, or a private citizen without a business, doesn't change those needs. I believe it's as important to set your next stage up for success as it was for you to succeed at your businesses. How would you feel about that?"

The three looked at one another and grinned. "Yes!" was the simultaneous and enthusiastic response. Ladybug, ever the organizer, asked, "Let's put it on the calendar and choose a meeting place. I knew I would miss you all and am so glad that I won't have to miss you because you will be beside me all the way far into the future."

Grasshopper nodded and said, "Same here. Let's use that first meeting to determine our goals and action steps. Then, we can just relax and enjoy our lunch for today."

"Great idea, Grasshopper!" said Bee. "Schedule that first accountability meeting, and then let me know how I can support you all. That will be your actionable step for the day. I am so happy to have had the experience of working with each of you. Thank you!"

And the Moral of the Story is... *"The only place success comes before work is in the dictionary." ~Vince Lombardi*

Whatever is worth doing is worth doing the right way. This could mean building your business to be a valuable asset for a buyer or the next generation of your family, as well as planning your evolution into the next phase of your life.

We all know of stories about people who work for years, build a business, and have a lovely family that he/she can't spend as much time with as they'd like while they are running the company. Finally, they close it, sell it, or pass it on. Six months later, they're dead. Shockingly, these people never had the chance to enjoy what they worked so hard to do. Travel, family, friends, and their interests are all left — unexplored, undiscovered, and unfinished.

So, what are you willing to do to prevent that from happening to you? Building wealth might be part of the equation for you. If so, how can you get your business positioned to become an asset? You can start by listing the factors of your business that add value in the eyes of a prospective buyer, investor, or to your successor. Next, list the factors that detract from the value of your business from another person's viewpoint. Look back and check to see when (if ever) the last time was that you conducted an internal or external audit, a valuation, and a market analysis for your industry. Do a deeper survey of your active clients/customers, as well as those who decided not to buy from your company.

Sit down with the management team to discuss market trends. Consider sharing at least some of the data that you've collected, including the valuation, with a select group of employees. Determine the elements that create value within the company through the eyes of your team. Many of you will hesitate to do this. However, we feel your team has information that is vital to the long-term success or even survival of the company. If you share that information, you have the opportunity to deliver feedback to the team, as well as direct their efforts to increase the value of the business.

It takes a lot of time and energy to create a company that is not dependent on the owner. It takes commitment to develop a management team that fills critical knowledge gaps and is empowered to think critically and make decisions based on the company's values, mission, and purpose. It takes time, energy, and commitment from every stakeholder to navigate the unexpected, the disruptions, and innovations that are part of any market.

One of our clients has been engaged in this process for almost a year. It appeared that a new hire would develop into just the right person to fill a key position. That right person is very important to the overall independence of the company from the owner. Unfortunately, the new hire declined the opportunity. So, it's back to the drawing board. While this is very discouraging to our client, we prepared for this possibility. We have time.

The recent pandemic devastated the economy and wreaked havoc on small businesses. My clients who had built up resilience with intention, along with a long-term strategy that included scenario planning, survived to recover. Those businesses that did not respond quickly did not revise their business models, plans for operating, and had no recovery plan other than hope. Hope is not a business, operations, or recovery plan. The number of business owners who had worked to create their well-funded retirements, and lost those businesses, was heartbreaking.

We joke with our financial planner that the word "retirement" should be retired. We prefer the word "evolution." There can be a lot of negative vibes when you use the word "retirement" with our peers. Yet, ignoring retirement, or counting the days until it arrives, are attitudes that leave a lot of room for failure.

What does that matter, you ask? Successfully preparing for, and thriving throughout retirement has huge financial, emotional, physical, and spiritual implications. The implications of failure in those areas are terrifying.

So, what should you do? We recommend to all of our clients that they engage a financial planner and advisor. Also, take care of your physical well-being. Most people understand the benefits of having a yearly physical check-up, but many of us struggle to follow the recommendations that come from those exams. One of our clients suffers from a chronic illness. For this person, coaching around health and well-being goals is as important as the strategic goals for the company.

The aspects of emotional and spiritual well-being can be trickier for many of our clients to tackle alone. Working with a coach who acts as your thought partner and transformation agent can be the proverbial "ace up your sleeve." This is your opportunity to apply the values, mission, and purpose that you brought into play when guiding the trajectory of your company to your next phase in life. After all, how can you enter into that next phase of life with enthusiasm, without actually working on mission and purpose?

In our story, Ladybug, Ant, and Grasshopper spent years working, building, and then curating the learning from each of their experiences. They were willing to share their experiences so that the others could learn from those lessons. The characters were willing to risk being vulnerable and transparent with external advisors to not only build their companies but also to build relationships within their companies and families, as well as with each other.

Sometimes an exit leads to retirement. We have had a lot of conversations with the family members of retired business owners, who ask us to please talk with their loved ones. He, or she, is wasting away in retirement. The challenge is that the person has to want the support. A lot of people feel like they should be able to figure things out on their own. Yet, they haven't been able to do so successfully. We would love the chance to work with these people to coach them through their transitions to their ultimate "evolution."

In the meantime, you have a series of journal prompts to begin to visualize your ideal exit. You can explore these answers in your journal or visit www.ascendcoachingsolutions.com for the downloadable PDF.

ASCEND
Coaching Solutions

Proposed Date of Ideal Exit:

What does your ideal exit look like?

What are the essential ingredients for a successful exit?

What do you anticipate are the greatest obstacles to your ideal exit?

Who are the key stakeholders in your exit? How will their roles change?

Who will be most impacted by this ideal exit? How might each respond?

What new skills will you need to exit successfully?

www.ascendcoachingsolutions.com

As we close this fable and our time together, we'd like to encourage you to consider the following:

- Expand your sense of self-awareness. Know your strengths, weaknesses, gifts, gaps, patterns of behavior, and blind spots. Know your values, mission, and purpose. Know your money story.
- Use a growth mindset. Learn every day. Identify and work with outside advisors, including a coach/mentor and an attorney and an accountant, for the duration of whatever it is you are trying to accomplish. You are one person, with one brain, and one perspective.
- Be ready. Plan, explore, discover, and experiment. Learn to identify the opportunities in your market or industry, and design your company's practices, systems, and processes accordingly. Invest in your people and in yourself.
- Build resilience. Reflect upon and curate the wisdom you and your team gain from each experience. Exercise those resilience muscles and teach your team to do the same. See failure as an opportunity. Challenges are an opportunity to lead, to experiment, and to design your response to whatever happens.

We've shared tools to equip you for this journey at the intersection of life and business. We believe that a better business sets you up for a better life. But, here's the thing — by practicing best practices every day, you build a better business and a better life. Well done, fable partner, well done!

REFERENCES

Aesop, and Heidi Holder. Aesop's Fables. New York: Viking Press, 1981.

Wickman, Gino. *Traction*. Kindle Edition. New York : BenBella Books, Inc., 2012.

Strategyzer's Business Model Canvas Plan: https://assets.strategyzer. com/assets/resources/the-business-model-canvas.pdf.

Bates, Mary. "Bumblebees Multitask — When the Stakes Are High," *Wired,* November 12, 2013, https://www.wired.com/2013/11/bumblebees-multitask-when-the-stakes-are-high/.

Toon, John. "Multi-Tasking Moths," *Georgia Tech Research Horizons,* Issue 2, 2015. https://rh.gatech.edu/features/multitasking-moths.

PwC's 2019 Family Business Survey, https://www.pwc.com/us/en/industries/private-company-services/library/family-business-survey.html

US Family Business Survey, "Creating stronger foundations for the future: How US family businesses can sustain their trust premium through digital transformations," *www.pwc.com › publicaciones › archivo › 2019/06 › 2...*

McDonald, Steven. "Why Customer Complaints Are Good For Your Business," 2013. Super Office. https://www.superoffice.com/blog/customer-complaints-good-for-business/ Last updated 10 July, 2020.

Parker, Richard. Quoted from *President of The Business Buyer Resource Center and author of How To Buy A Good Business At A Great Price©,* 2020. The Business Buyer Resource Center. https://www.diomo.com/industry-statistics-that-every-buyer-needs-to-know.html

Jackson, Annifer. "Why do up to 90% of Mergers and Acquisitions Fail?" January 2015. Business Chief, EU. https://www.businesschief.eu/finance/why-do-90-mergers-and-acquisitions-fail. Quoted from *Nine Feet Tall,* McMorris, Esther.

"The B2B Elements of Value," Bain & Company, infographic. March 08, 2018.https://www.bain.com/insights/eov-b2c-infographic/

"The B2C Elements of Value," Bain & Company, infographic. March 08, 2018. https://www.bain.com/insights/eov-b2c-infographic/

Ellis, R., Saloner, Garth, Silverman, Amanda. "Circles, Lifecycle of a New Venture," 2008. Stanford Graduate School of Business. https://www.gsb.stanford.edu/faculty-research/case-studies/circles-lifecycle-new-venture

Pest World for Kids. "Ants," Pestworld.org, 2018. https://pestworldforkids.org/pest-guide/ants/

Deane, Michael T. "The Top 6 Reasons New Businesses Fail," June 25, 2019. Investopedia. https://www.investopedia.com/financial-edge/1010/top-6-reasons-new-businesses-fail.aspx

Robbins, Tony, "5 Major Pain Points and how to solve them: Get ahead of these pitfalls and keep your growth steady." Tony Robbins. https://www.tonyrobbins.com/career-business/cultural-problems-of-scale/

Bajweb. "10 Strongest Insects in the World," http://www.mytop10.bajweb.com/10-strongest-insects-in-the-world/

Small Business Administration (SBA), https://www.sba.gov/

Moran, Brian. *The 12 Week Year*. Hardback Edition. Wiley; 1 edition, May 20, 2013.

Interaction Design Foundation, https://www.interaction-design.org/

Iron Mountain®, https://www.ironmountain.com/

Science Learning Hub – Pokapū Akoranga Pūtaiao, The University of Waikato Te Whare Wānanga o Waikato, "Insect Antennae," ©

2007-2020. https://www.sciencelearn.org.nz/resources/2756-insect-antennae

Merhar, Christina, "Employee Retention - The Real Cost of Losing an Employee," 2013. PeopleKeep. https://www.peoplekeep.com/blog/employee-retention-the-real-cost-of-losing-an-employee (Updated June 2, 2020)

UP Professional Solutions, https://www.uppros.com/

Introducing the Eisenhower Matrix, © 2011-2017 by EISENHOWER, a registered trademark by FTL3. All rights reserved. https://www.eisenhower.me/eisenhower-matrix/

Wayne Gretzky Quote sourced from Brainy Quote: https://www.brainyquote.com/authors/wayne-gretzky-quotes

NFL is the trademark of the National Football League. https://www.nfl.com/

ESPN is the trademark of ESPN, Inc. https://www.espn.com/

Vince Lombardi Quote sourced from Brainy Quote: https://www.brainyquote.com/quotes/vince_lombardi_109282

"The Three Components of Family Governance," 12 November 2001. Harvard Business School. https://hbswk.hbs.edu/item/the-three-components-of-family-governance.

Trevor Blake, *Secrets To a Successful Startup: A Recession-Proof Guide to Starting, Surviving, & Thriving in Your Own Venture*. Kindle Edition. New World Library, January 28, 2020.

NOTES

Quiz: Are You An Ant, A Grasshopper, Or An Anthopper?

1. Systemize - "Systemizing involves clearly identifying what those core processes are and integrating them into a fully functioning machine." (Wick-man, Gino. Traction (p. 22). BenBella Books, Inc.. Kindle Edition.)
2. Structure - Your company needs to be organized in a way that reduces complexity and creates accountability. In addition, this structure should also be designed to boost you to the next level. (Wickman, Gino. Traction (p. 22). BenBella Books, Inc.. Kindle Edition.)

1. Make a Mountain Out of an Anthill

3. Strategyzer's Business Plan Canvas Model: https://assets.strategyzer.com/assets/resources/the-business-model-canvas.pdf.
4. https://www.gsb.stanford.edu/faculty-research/case-studies/circles-lifecycle-new-venture

2. Build Your Colony and Design Your Cloud

5. *Investopedia* published these statistics from Michael T. Deane's article, "The Top 6 Reasons New Businesses Fail," dated June 25, 2019.
6. https://www.tonyrobbins.com/career-business/cultural-problems-of-scale/

4. Keep Your Eyes on the Prize

7. Turnover seems to vary by wage and role of employee. For example, a CAP study found average costs to replace an employee are: 16 percent of annual salary for high-turnover, low-paying jobs (earning under $30,000 a year). For example, the cost to replace a $10/hour retail employee would be $3,328. CAP Study

CPSIA information can be obtained
at www.ICGtesting.com
Printed in the USA
LVHW081302030921
696883LV00021B/1011/J

9 781950 306480